FAIR NOT FLAT

FAIR

NOT

FLAT

**HOW TO MAKE THE TAX SYSTEM
BETTER AND SIMPLER**

Edward J. McCaffery

THE UNIVERSITY OF CHICAGO PRESS • CHICAGO AND LONDON

Edward J. McCaffery is the Maurice Jones Jr. Professor of Law at the University of Southern California Law School and Visiting Professor of Law and Economics at the California Institute of Technology. He is the author of *Taxing Women* (1997), also published by the University of Chicago Press.

The University of Chicago Press, Chicago 60637
The University of Chicago Press, Ltd., London
© 2002 by Edward J. McCaffery
All rights reserved. Published 2002
Printed in the United States of America
11 10 09 08 07 06 05 04 03 02   1 2 3 4 5

ISBN: 0-226-55560-7 (cloth)

Library of Congress Cataloging-in-Publication Data

McCaffery, Edward J.
    Fair not flat : how to make the tax system better and
simpler / Edward J. McCaffery.
        p.   cm.
    Includes bibliographical references and index.
    ISBN 0-226-55560-7 (cloth : alk. paper)
    1. Spendings tax—United States. 2. Income tax—United
States. 3. Taxation—United States. I. Title.

HJ5715.U6 M22 2002
336.2′05′0973—dc21

                                        2001043391

To Cathleen and Allegra, with love

CONTENTS

TABLES AND FIGURES

TABLES

FIGURES

ACKNOWLEDGMENTS

This book has been a long time in coming. It is the product of many years of thinking, reading, writing, and talking about tax, with many persons and in many forms and forums. It would be foolish to attempt to list all of my personal debts here. But fools rush in, and no one but a fool would write a book about tax reform intended for the masses. And so with apologies to those I am no doubt omitting—and with the clear understanding that no one I mention agrees with all or even most of what I have to say in the book—I thank Scott Altman, Mike Alvarez, Jon Beckman, Chuck Davenport, Joel Newman, Jonathan Schwartz, Laurence Seidman, Joe Spieler, Kirk Stark, Leo Weigman, and Larry Zelenak for their comments on the manuscript and for various forms of encouragement in producing it.

I owe an older debt to my tax professors at Harvard Law School: Louis Kaplow, Bernie Wolfman, and especially Bill Andrews, whose wonderful work on consumption taxation got me started on this long and winding road. I cannot blame my education or my educators for any mistakes that follow.

My work on the estate tax in particular has brought me into contact with several people affiliated with think tanks or other organizations, generally in Washington, D.C., who have been helpful in furthering my thinking about tax, including Bill Beach at the Heritage Foundation, Bill Gale at Brookings, Douglas Holtz-Eakin at the National Tax Association, Steve Moore at Cato, and Pat Soldano of the Center for the Study of Taxation. Senator Bob Packwood has been a source of inspiration ever since I testified before his Senate Finance Committee about the estate tax. Richard Wagner and I wrote a fun piece together arguing against the "death tax," and I learned just from working with Dick.

Josh Galper and Mark Alexander of the inspired if unsuccessful Bill Bradley for President campaign were supportive friends and colleagues during my brief stint as an informal advisor to the cause.

Various journalists of the old-fashioned print and the new electronic media have become good friends, both sources of ideas and outlets for my expressions of them: Hanno Beck of the *Progress Report,* David Cay Johnston of the *New York Times,* Amity Shlaes of the *Financial Times,* and Lindsay Sobel of *American Prospect Online.* Lindsay arranged a most informative debate with Chuck Collins of United for a Fair Economy about the estate tax repeal efforts.

I was blessed to begin this project under one wonderful dean at USC Law School, Scott Bice, and to conclude it under another, Matt Spitzer; I continued to teach part time at Caltech during my writing, under the ever helpful guidance of John Ledyard, chair of the Division of the Humanities and Social Sciences; and I spent a happy term visiting crosstown at UCLA Law School, for which I owe thanks to Dean Jon Varat. All of these persons and their institutions, especially USC Law School, have supported me financially during my quixotic quest to improve America's tax laws.

The librarians at USC, under the leadership of Albert Brecht, were their usual extraordinary selves. I thank Darin Fox, Diana Jaque, Hazel Lord, Jennifer Murray, Wendy Nobunaga, Brian Raphael, William Smith, and Leonette Williams for going beyond the call of duty to help with my sundry ill-timed and burdensome requests.

Tim Lan and Negin Mirmirani provided first-class research assistance throughout.

Shirly Kennedy provided first-class administrative assistance, also throughout.

My old friends at the University of Chicago Press, Geoff Huck and Leslie Keros, were once again patient, understanding, and most helpful. I learned as I was completing this book that the wonderful copy editor of *Taxing Women,* Wilma Ebbitt, had recently passed away, and I want to take these words to honor her memory. Wilma was irreplaceable. But Meg Cox performed magical feats of wonder with the manuscript for the present effort, spinning straw into something at least approaching gold. Joan Huh and Mayer Nazarian also helped with copyediting and proofreading.

Finally, and most personally, I thank my loving daughters, Cathleen and Allegra, the best reasons I know to care about the future.

Time for a Change

"Taxes," said rich dad. "You're taxed when you earn. You're taxed when you spend. You're taxed when you save. You're taxed when you die."

"Why do people let the government do that to them?"

"The rich don't," said rich dad with a smile. "The poor and the middle class do. I'll bet you that I earn more than your dad, yet he pays more in taxes."

"How can that be?" I asked. As a 9-year-old boy, that made no sense to me.

—Robert T. Kiyosaki (with Sharon L. Lechter), *Rich Dad, Poor Dad*

I BEGIN WITH TWO FACTS ABOUT AMERICA TODAY. ONE, our tax system is a disgrace, and has been so for decades. The way we tax is complicated, inefficient, and unfair. Yet whenever elected officials in Washington actually try to do something about tax, they tinker at best. At worst, they make the system even more annoying. We need fundamental, comprehensive tax reform, not ad hoc tinkering.

Two, there is a widening gap between the rich and the not-rich in this country.

It may surprise many readers to learn that there is a deep connection between these two facts. Tax as it is today is a cause of the wealth gap. Tax as it could be tomorrow would narrow it. That's what this book is about: a proposal to make the tax system better

1

and fairer so that we can get to a model of class teamwork, not class conflict, in this great nation. Right now we're a long way from realizing that goal.

This is not a tax-planning book. It is a book about change—long overdue change. The problem can be simply stated: Under the current American tax system, if you have wealth, you don't need to pay tax anymore; taxes have become voluntary. But if you are like most ordinary wage earners laboring to earn their keep, you have precious little choice but to pay your distant Uncle Sam first before you get money for your daily bread. Tax is a nightmare from which you cannot escape.

Tax today is fundamentally set against work and savings: it makes it hard for people to build up wealth in the first place. Yet once you have wealth, whether you earned it or were given it, you are home—and tax—free. Life on top is very good, with ever new and ever more expensive luxuries for you to enjoy. And with very basic tax planning, you need never pay tax on your lavish lifestyle. But if you are not rich, these are difficult times. Life is stressful as you live from paycheck to paycheck, never seeming to get ahead. And yet you are taxed at every turn.

Books like the best-seller *Rich Dad, Poor Dad* chronicle the divide between the rich and the not-rich and give advice—often not very good advice—about how individuals can bridge the gap and get to the promised land of riches without taxation. This book takes a different tack. It proceeds from the premise that something is wrong with the picture. I will explain why that picture needs to be fixed and how it can be—for all Americans. I will answer the question the nine-year-old boy posed to Rich Dad, about how it has come to be that under our federal system tax falls on wage earners but not on wealth holders. And I will recommend fundamental changes in order to get tax right.

TROUBLE IN RIVER CITY

The American tax system, including all federal, state, and local taxes, is huge. It takes in over one-third of all dollars produced in this country each year. But the size of the tax burden is not my complaint, nor, by and large, is it that of the American people, who understand

ON *RICH DAD, POOR DAD* AND
OTHER BEST-SELLERS

In text boxes throughout this book, I use fictional characters, real-life stories, and contemporary best-sellers to illustrate ideas in the main text. I also begin many of the chapters with quotations from popular business books. These volumes give an interesting perspective on contemporary America. They reflect the general state of knowledge about financial facts of life, and they capture many of our common hopes and dreams.

The best-selling *Rich Dad, Poor Dad: What the Rich Teach Their Kids about Money—That the Poor and Middle Class Do Not!* by Robert T. Kiyosaki with Sharon Lechter is typical of this genre. At times condescending in its attitude toward the "poor and middle class," more often vague—and occasionally wrong—in its basic financial advice, *Rich Dad, Poor Dad* nonetheless conveys two vital truths about economic life in the United States today. One, there are many ways that the rich can get richer. Two, the poor and middle class must labor away just to hold steady and pay their bills. Kiyosaki's aim is to advise his readers on how to get rich so that they can win under the existing rules. My aim is to recommend a change in those rules to make it easier for the poor and middle classes to become rich in the first place, and to make it harder for the rich to avoid being taxed as they live a lavish lifestyle in the second place.

full well that taxes pay for important public goods and services, including Social Security, Medicare, schools, police, roads, national defense, and so on. There's more to talk about with regard to a tax system than its size. Whatever level of taxation we have, there are important questions about the way we tax.

Trouble is, the way we tax today is complicated, inefficient, and, most importantly, unfair. Rich Dad points to the starkest aspect of our tax system's unfairness: the surprisingly obscure fact that paying tax has become virtually voluntary for the growing number of Americans who have made a fortune for themselves and can comfortably live out the rest of their days on the yield from their property holdings. Meanwhile, workers—lower-, middle-, and upper-middle-class citizens—are taxed on all sides, often at combined rates of 50 percent or higher, with nowhere to hide. America has developed an onerous wage-tax system with massive holes when it comes to taxing wealth and its products. That shouldn't make sense to any of us.

What makes even less sense is the fact that things are staying the way they are. It isn't all that difficult, conceptually, to fix the system—to make tax simpler, fairer, and more efficient. My aim in this book is to explain how to get tax right. It's surprisingly simple.

PLENTY OF BLAME TO GO AROUND

There are plenty of reasons for the mess we're in. To begin with, it's not practical to change a large and important system like tax without popular support. But it's hard to gain that support when so few Americans understand the deep incoherence of tax today. The basic form of the tax system has become mind-numbingly difficult to discern. It's hard even to sense the existing problems. Popular understanding of tax looks to statistics that feature only reported income and therefore hide the root problem: the ability of the wealthy to easily, and perfectly legally, live off the fruits of *un*reported income.

People need help to understand tax. But no one seems ready, willing, or able to help them. The media lack the time and resources to figure it all out. And academics, who do have the time and talent, haven't been much help. Consider some basic facts. The largest overall tax in America, and the focus of most academic analysis, is the federal personal income tax. Yet most Americans pay more in payroll taxes than they do in income taxes. Further, what we call an income tax isn't really an income tax at all. An income tax is supposed to tax income, whatever its source: whether it comes from wages or as a return on investments. But our so-called income tax is extremely inconsistent when it comes to taxing the latter type of income. The "income" tax is in fact far closer to a wage tax, one that taxes labor earnings alone. Rich people don't have to report their increases in wealth to the federal tax collector, yet they can borrow against their wealth and spend away. Meanwhile, wage earners see both income and payroll taxes come out of their paychecks before the checks can be cashed. That's reality today for most of us. Still, academics continue to debate the relative merits of income versus consumption taxes, oblivious to the fact that what we have is an incoherent mixture of the two. Scholars rarely comment on how bad the status quo is or support sensible changes to it; they often fail even to note the growing role of the payroll tax in the bigger picture of tax. Many academics are quicker to point out the many difficulties of change—any change—than the deep structural problems in the way things are. Few try to explain to ordinary people the basic flaws of the tax system or sensible alternatives to it.

Wealthy people and their well-paid tax advisors are even less help. These fortunate few are doing just fine under the status quo. They have no interest in change. Most people who know enough about tax to see its deep flaws are making a good living by exploiting those flaws. Tax is simply too important to leave to the few people who already happen to understand it.

Politicians seem particularly unable or unwilling to fix the mess. Whenever they have the chance, politicians do things to help their favored constituencies. Republicans aim to cut taxes for the wealthiest few, helping the rich to get richer. Democrats aim to do as little about taxes as possible, preferring continued spending programs and minor complicating changes to fundamental reform. It's difficult to get anywhere with the inside-the-beltway crowd, because what they want is out of step with what the average American citizen needs and deserves: a better, simpler, fairer tax system.

ME AND MY BOOK

As a tax lawyer, an economist, and a professor, I have been thinking, writing, testifying, and lecturing about tax reform for more than a decade. My mission is to help make the tax laws more sensible and fair for ordinary Americans. My ideas have helped to further public discussion about the "marriage penalty" and about the ills of the so-called death tax. But I have been frustrated with what politicians have and have not done with my ideas: they're interested in sound bites, not real reform.

Hope exists; mine persists. There is a better way to tax. I believe that America should have a progressive consumption tax, one that falls consistently on spending, not on work or savings. There is no reason to tax work and savings directly. Nor is there any reason to raise taxes for the middle class in order to pay for tax reductions for the rich, as the common flat-tax plans would do. America should have a tax system whose basic principles we can all understand: a fair not flat one.

I did not write this book for politicians, academics, or the wealthy. Instead I am taking my ideas straight to the people. I wrote this book to answer the nine-year-old's question in *Rich Dad, Poor Dad*, to explain how tax today works and why it is badly wrong. And I wrote it to propose a simpler, fairer tax system.

THE BASIC PLAN

My proposal is simple:

- change the inconsistent income tax to a consistent spending tax by granting an unlimited deduction for savings and making other logical corrections
- repeal the so-called death tax
- keep tax rates progressive
- reduce the paperwork burden that most Americans now face

The result is, in essence, a progressive national sales tax. I call it the Fair Not Flat Tax.

The Fair Not Flat Tax can take several different forms. I will emphasize one that features a broad consumption tax such as a sales or value-added tax with a rebate for low-end spenders and a supplemental personal consumption tax for high-end ones. Roughly speaking, a family of four will pay no tax on its first $20,000 of spending and a 10 percent tax on its next $60,000. Only a minority of families, those that spend more than $80,000 a year on themselves, will have to fill out tax forms and pay higher rates under the supplemental consumption tax.

I readily admit that my numbers are illustrative and are only estimates. I mean this book to be general and highly readable. I will not engage in long, technical discussions about precise rates and numbers, adding fuel to think-tank fires. Complexity can wait. The devil may indeed dwell in the details, but we first need to find an angel or two in the abstractions that govern tax. It's time to get the basic principles of tax down right.

WHY THE PLAN IS FAIR

The Fair Not Flat Tax is fair because it rests on a simple and consistent principle: tax people on what they spend, not on what they earn or save. The Fair Not Flat Tax sticks to this principle. It does not contain a death tax for the simple reason that dead people don't spend. The Fair Not Flat Tax instead taxes heirs when they spend inherited wealth. It is a far better, far more consistent tax on the wealthy, of both the first and later generations, than the ineffective system we now have.

The Fair Not Flat Tax is fair because it assigns a lower rate of tax to spending on life's necessities—like food, clothing, shelter, medical care, and education—than to spending on life's ordinary pleasures, and it assigns the highest tax rate to spending on life's luxuries.

The Fair Not Flat Tax is fair because, unlike most of the common flat-tax plans, it does not raise tax rates on the middle class to pay for tax reductions for the rich.

The Fair Not Flat Tax is fair because it does not require most Americans to fill out complicated and intimidating tax forms every year.

And, finally, the Fair Not Flat Tax is fair because it represents the best practical expression of current American attitudes toward tax and wealth. Or so I aim to convince you.

A NOTE TO READERS

I have tried to write a simple book about a complex subject. I have skipped the usual academic devices of footnotes and such, and I have deliberately kept my text and examples simple and straightforward. I know from experience that many questions and objections will come up in your mind as you read. To help answer these, I have gathered up many and put them in a Questions and Comments section at the end. This has its own table of contents that you can browse to find the topic you have in mind. I have also included a glossary of key technical terms and a guide to other books on tax policy that you might find of interest.

I hope you will enjoy this book. More important, I hope you will get motivated to help fix the mess we've gotten ourselves into. Tax needs your help.

ONE

Tax Basics

Every time people try to punish the rich, the rich don't simply comply, they react. They have the money, power, and intent to change things. They do not just sit there and voluntarily pay more taxes. They search for ways to minimize their tax burden. They hire smart attorneys and accountants, and persuade politicians to change laws or create legal loopholes. They have the resources to effect change. . . . The poor and middle class do not have the same resources. They sit there and let the government's needles enter their arm and allow the blood donation to begin.

—Kiyosaki, *Rich Dad, Poor Dad*

TO BUILD A NEW TAX SYSTEM, WE SHOULD FIRST UNDERstand the current one. This sounds intimidating, but it need not be. A few basic ideas help to make the big picture of tax clear.

Tax has building blocks, just like any complex subject. There are four particularly important ones in tax: the taxable unit, the tax base, the rate structure, and the timing of tax. Who pays tax? On what? How much? When? These practical questions lie at the core of all tax systems.

Bases and rates are the typical concerns of tax policymakers. After all, it makes sense to start by thinking about what we are taxing, and to what extent. But I have learned from years of thinking about tax that timing may be the most essential building block of all. Making a fair choice about the tax base and rate structure involves understanding *when* in people's lives they are being and should be taxed: when they work, save, borrow, or spend. I'll return again and again to this timing theme: it will help us see what's wrong with the way things are and what's right with the Fair Not Flat Tax.

The *who* question matters, too. Should individuals, married couples, or households pay the tax? Odd and often conflicting decisions about the taxpayer unit have put great pressure on two-earner households, now the norm for married couples in America. The question of who pays tax—and the unfairness of the current answer to it—was central to my first book, *Taxing Women*. It will, however, largely remain offstage in this one.

Let's turn then to the *what* question. A tax's base is what is being taxed. An income tax, for example, has income for its base. The base of a sales tax is the value of whatever goods and services the tax covers. The base of a property tax is the value of property. A payroll tax has wages for its base. And so on.

Now let's turn to the *how much* question. A tax's rate structure defines the levels at which the base gets taxed. The simplest rate structure is a flat one. Most sales taxes have such a structure; they have a single rate—say 10 percent. For every dollar spent on covered goods or services, ten cents is paid out in taxes.

The income tax has a more complicated rate structure. Different levels of income are taxed at different marginal rates. The first $10,000 of income may not be taxed at all. The tax rate for this range is zero percent; the taxpayer is in the zero bracket. The next $20,000 of income—which moves an individual taxpayer from $10,000 to $30,000 in total income—may be taxed at a 15 percent marginal tax rate. For any income above $30,000, the taxpayer may enter the 30 percent bracket—she'll be taxed at a 30 percent rate on her additional, or marginal, income. Note that when you enter a new marginal rate bracket, that rate does not apply to *all* of your income, as people often believe. A taxpayer who makes $50,000 in this running example will pay $9,000 in tax: $0 on her first $10,000; plus $3,000, or 15 percent, of her next $20,000; plus $6,000, or 30 percent, of her final $20,000.

These ascending rate brackets produce progressivity in the income tax. The rich pay a higher percentage of their income in tax than the not-rich. Or so it is supposed to work. You see this type of rate structure in the tax-rate tables provided along with the instructions to the 1040 tax form every year. I will discuss tax rates more in chapter 5, after we've resolved the base, or *what,* question.

THE RELATION BETWEEN BASE AND RATE

Bases and rates stand in a simple relation:

$$\text{Base} \times \text{Rate} = \text{Tax Owed}$$

This simple relation helps to illustrate a simple point about tax that is often overlooked:

The tax base and its rate structure are two separate matters.

We need to know both the base and the rate in order to figure out how much tax is owed.

There are, of course, sound reasons to combine the discussions of tax base and rate. The more inclusive the tax base is—the more things that are taxed—the lower the rate can be, all else equal. This poses a problem for advocates of a national sales tax. If we shrink the sales tax base by carving out exceptions for food and other necessities, the tax rate on what is left has to increase to yield the needed revenue. I'll address this problem later, when I develop the details of the Fair Not Flat Tax. For now, although there are reasons to connect the tax's base and its rate structure in theory, it is important to understand that these two building blocks are logically separate. "What?" and "How much?" are different questions. I'll treat each of them in turn.

DEFINING THE BASE

The first tax base I'll examine is income, for the income tax is what most Americans think of when they think of tax and tax reform, even though the payroll tax is the more burdensome one for most Americans.

What is "income"? Most academic and political discussions begin with the Haig-Simons definition of income, named after the academics Robert Haig and Henry Simons, both of whom wrote in the first half of the twentieth century. Their definition is so basic that it's hard to see why anyone would fuss over it, yet simple principles often underlie complex structures. Simons used many more words to express his definition of income, but in essence it says this:

$$\text{Income} = \text{Consumption} + \text{Savings}$$

To restate more generally:

$$\text{Sources} = \text{Uses}$$

The left-hand side of the equation, Sources or Income, stands for inflows of wealth. Think of filling out an income tax return. You first list all of the sources of income you had for the year. You begin with your wages, generally found on W-2 forms. You add any interest you received from bank accounts or mutual funds. You also add profits you had from any business you ran on the side, proceeds from the sale of something you owned, and so forth. You are tallying your inflows, or sources, to come up with a gross income amount.

During the year you put all of your income to some use. This is what the right-hand side of the equation, Uses or Consumption + Savings, represents. All of your inflows were matched, somewhere along the line, by outflows. Consumption + Savings simply describes, in broad terms, the possible uses of income. Consumption and savings are mutually exclusive and all encompassing. They account for every penny you had available during any particular period of time.

This leads to a second restatement:

$$\text{All income is either spent or not spent.}$$

This restatement shows just how commonsensical the Haig-Simons definition is. You either spend a given sum of money—that is, you consume it—or you don't spend it. Not spending income is saving. So you either spend or save all available resources. Items such as gifts and losses can be fit into this equation readily enough: we can treat either as a form of spending or dissaving, for example. But in keeping with the spirit of this book, I'll skip over such details and focus on the bigger picture. It turns out that the surprisingly obvious facts we've learned so far lead to important insights into tax policy—

ideas that are often overlooked, misunderstood, or ignored, even by supposed experts in tax.

THREE PRINCIPLES OF TAX

Consider three principles that follow logically from the basic definition of income. One:

**You can think about the tax base in terms of either the sources
or the uses of income.**

When you think of an income tax, you tend to think of the various sources of income. You imagine filling out a tax return where you add together different inflows to come up with a gross figure. Then you subtract whatever the law allows—items like mortgage interest or charitable contributions—to get a net figure, and you pay tax on that.

But the first principle shows that you don't have to think of an income tax this way. If you instead add together all of the uses of your inflows, you would come up with the same amount, by definition. Consider a basic fact of arithmetic. You can interchange the two sides of an equation:

$$2 = 1 + 1$$
$$1 + 1 = 2$$

So it is with the definition of income:

Income = Consumption + Savings
Consumption + Savings = Income

Powerful insights follow from this simple fact. Consider, for example, various subtractions that the tax law now allows. You might think of some, like business-expense deductions, as proper because they are appropriate adjustments on the sources, or inflow, side of the equation. Imagine a small-business owner who sells $50,000 worth of shoes. Suppose she had to pay $20,000 to the manufacturer to acquire the shoes in the first place. It would be absurd to tax her on the full $50,000, ignoring her expenses. Her net income is only $30,000: the $50,000 in gross receipts minus the $20,000 cost of the shoes sold. The law simply has to allow deductions for reasonable business expenses to get to a fair and accurate picture of income.

On the other hand, you might think of other deductions, like those for medical expenses or charitable contributions, as special deviations from the income tax because they have nothing at all to do with the sources of income. But the first principle gives us a new way to think about tax. Now you can see such deductions as appropriate adjustments to the uses side of the equation.

Once you see that the combination of all consumption and all savings makes up the income tax base, you can ask whether or not this should be so. Just as we carve out necessities like food and medicine from the base of most local sales taxes, we carve out exceptions from the consumption and savings that are part of the income tax's base.

JACK AND JILL WENT UP THE HILL

To help us to better understand the Haig-Simons definition of income and how it can be used, let's meet the first in a series of imaginary taxpayers, Jack and Jill. Each earns $30,000 in salary. On the sources side their incomes are equal. You might therefore think it fair for Jack and Jill to be taxed alike. But suppose that Jack suffers a terrible accident and incurs $10,000 in life-saving medical expenses, and Jill does not. Are the two still equal in terms of the kinds of consumption and savings choices—the uses side of the Haig-Simons definition—they have available to them? We could say that Jack really only has $20,000 to spend as he sees fit, that this is the amount that is fair and appropriate to tax him on. If we had a national sales tax, we might choose to exclude the cost of vital medical services from it. Why then should an income tax, which also includes consumption in its base, include such emergency items?

A second principle:

Most of the income tax's problems relate to its inconsistent treatment of savings.

An income tax is supposed to tax all consumption and all savings. Yet the taxing of savings under the income tax has been erratic at best. There are plenty of holes in our system's taxation of savings, including, but by no means limited to, contributions to Individual Retirement Accounts (IRAs) and qualified pension plans such as 401(k)s. I'll discuss these gaps much more fully in the next chapter when we consider what's wrong with an income tax. For now, I want to underscore that we don't have a consistent income tax and never have had one. What we have is in part a consumption tax, for a consumption tax is any broad-based tax—one falling on inflows or outflows—that does not directly include savings in its base.

We can see this by simply rearranging the definition of income. Subtracting savings from both sides, we get the following:

$$\text{Income} - \text{Savings} = \text{Consumption}$$

When we turn this around, we see

$$\text{Consumption} = \text{Income} - \text{Savings}$$

This leads to a third principle:

Any "income" tax that systematically deducts savings from income is in fact a consumption tax.

Because the inconsistencies of the income tax relate more often than not to its failure to tax savings—the income tax allows a deduction for large amounts of savings and fails to reach other forms of it—the next point should not surprise you much: we basically have a consumption tax system today. But because we haven't put a great deal of conscious planning or forethought into getting where we are, it's a mess.

TWO FORMS OF CONSUMPTION TAX

There are two forms of consumption tax: one that is imposed when money is first earned and another that is imposed later, when the money is spent. If the tax rate is the same at the two times, then the two types of consumption tax lead to an identical result.

A simple numerical example helps to make the point. Suppose that the thrifty Ant earns $200, there is a 50 percent tax rate, and the interest rate she can earn in a savings account is 10 percent per year. If Ant is taxed up front on her wages, she's left with $100. She saves this money. In Year 1 it grows by 10 percent, or $10, to $110, and Ant keeps saving. In Year 2 Ant's money grows again by 10 percent, this time $11, to $121. She spends this.

In another scenario Ant won't be taxed until she spends. She therefore gets to save the entire $200 she earns. In Year 1 this grows by 10 percent, or $20, to $220. In Year 2 Ant gets another 10 percent, now $22, for a total of $242. When she goes to spend, the government imposes its 50 percent tax, cutting her $242 in half—to $121. Ant has the same amount to spend in the postpaid as in the prepaid tax model.

There is no magic here. Simple algebra proves that under the same tax rate the two forms of consumption tax must lead to the same place. Tax experts tend to call the first tax a prepaid consumption tax and the second a postpaid one. But you can just as easily understand each in terms of its primary real world examples: the former is a wage or payroll tax, the latter a sales or spending tax. Because, as I will argue, spending is a better, fairer time to tax than wage-earning is, the Fair Not Flat Tax chooses the second consumption tax model. It is a postpaid consumption, or spending, tax.

A PICTURE OF A TYPICAL LIFE

Prepaid and postpaid consumption taxes lead to the same result, given a constant tax rate. But the results differ under variable or progressive rates. The choice comes down to this: What's a fairer time to make a decision about how much to tax, when money comes into a household or when it goes out?

The Fair Not Flat Tax is designed as a consistent, postpaid consumption tax because I believe that spending is a better activity to tax than earning. One way to understand this is through the perspective of an individual earner. Look at figure 1.1. The dotted line represents a typical earnings pattern: the majority of us earn most of our money over a limited period of our lives, say from our early twenties to our mid-sixties. Yet we spend in a much more even way. This is what the solid line represents.

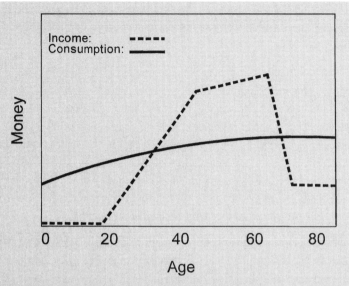

Figure 1.1 Income and Consumption over a Lifetime

Because our parents support us during childhood, in a sense we borrow to consume early in life; later, we must save to consume after we retire. We then have to overearn in our middle years to pay off the debts of our youth and to provide for the needs of our old age. A progressive tax on inflows—like an income or prepaid consumption tax—therefore seems unfair: it heavily taxes the high midlife earner, even if she is a thrifty soul, like Ant, who lives moderately at all times. (A progressive tax on inflows is even more unfair to people who have only a few good income years to provide for their whole lifetimes—like some artists and athletes.) A consistent postpaid tax, on the other hand, falls on our voluntary choice of spending level, not on the much more erratic profile of our earnings—it chooses to tax at a better, fairer time. It spreads the tax burden across our lifetimes, just as borrowing and savings decisions spread out our earnings across our lifetimes.

PAYROLL TAXES

Speaking of payroll taxes, for most American taxpayers—some 75 percent of them, in fact—the largest single tax is not the income tax. It's the federal payroll tax—the contributions withheld from both employer and employee for Social Security and Medicare. Rich Dad knows this:

> The No. 1 expense for most people is taxes. Many people think it's the income tax, but for most Americans their highest tax is Social Security. As an employee, it appears as if the Social Security tax combined with the Medicare tax is roughly 7.5 percent, but it's really 15 percent since the employer must match the Social Security amount. In essence, it is money the employer cannot pay you. On top of that, you still have to pay income tax on the amount deducted from your wages for Social Security tax, income you never receive because it went directly to Social Security through withholding.

To clear up one common misperception, Social Security and Medicare "contributions" are actually taxes. Many Americans think that these moneys are set aside for them, for their own personal retirement plans. It isn't so. Social Security operates as a pay-as-you-go system: the government collects money from current workers and immediately pays it out to current retirees. In other words, the government has a spending need, and it meets this need with a mandatory extraction. That's a tax. We could, in theory, use other taxes to meet the revenue need. When George W. Bush proposed a $1.6 trillion tax cut in the first month of his presidency, he was saying that the government could do perfectly fine without that sum over the next decade. He could easily have recommended a payroll tax cut instead of an income and estate tax one. The government's balance sheet would have looked no different for the switch.

As Rich Dad points out, the payroll tax is also double what it appears to be. Social Security and Medicare combined take 7.65 percent of a worker's wages until they reach a ceiling that is now roughly $80,000 as I write. After that the Social Security share ceases, and only the Medicare tax, at 1.45 percent, is collected. But for both Social Security and Medicare, the employer must match the employee's payments. This is money that the employer could have paid the employee if it weren't for the tax.

Once again a simple example helps. Suppose Poor Dad took a job paying $10,000. His employer would take $765 out of his paycheck for federal payroll taxes. But the employer would have to pay an additional $765 to Washington. On earnings of $10,000 the employer would send $1,530 to the government under the mandatory exaction scheme—money that might otherwise have gone to Poor Dad. That's a 15.3 percent tax any way you look at it. Economists and Rich Dad agree on this one.

The federal payroll tax system ought to loom large in any accurate picture of the status quo. This tax, alone among major American taxes, has never been cut. What's particularly unfortunate is that the federal payroll tax system is an odd and regressive one: the poor and middle classes pay more, as a percent of their earnings, than the rich do. The tax starts in at the very first dollar of wages and continues until wages hit $80,000; then it drops to the Medicare portion alone (2.9 percent combined employer and employee share). Just about every man, woman, and child who works in America must pay this. There are no deductions for family size, medical expenses, or anything else. When a second earner, typically the wife, enters the workforce, she gets no tax break even though her Social Security benefits are generally tied to her husband's: she's usually paying a pure tax, with no increase in what she'll ever receive back in benefits. Hardly anyone in America seems aware of these facts. The payroll tax is hidden behind its "contribution" label, the trick of the employer's share, and the fact that no one needs to fill out any payroll tax forms and face the pain directly.

DEBT

One final bit of basic tax information will equip you well for the intellectual journey ahead: different tax systems treat borrowing, or debt, differently.

An income tax does not include borrowing in its base. Borrowing causes no change in the borrower's net wealth because the asset of cash is matched by the liability of an IOU. In terms of the Haig-Simons definition, although you have more money to spend or save when you borrow, you also have negative savings—in the form of the debt—to offset that. Under a consistent income tax, you must repay the principal amount of debt with after-tax, or nondeductible, dollars.

A prepaid consumption, or wage, tax treats debt as an income tax does—by ignoring it. You don't pay Social Security tax when you borrow, and you don't get out of paying the tax when you use your wages to pay off the lender.

A postpaid consumption tax that falls on spending, not work or savings, is different. Such a tax includes the proceeds of debt in its base, then allows a deduction for the repayment of debt. A consistent postpaid consumption tax puts the tax burden squarely on the act of spending, whether this spending is financed by earnings, savings, debt, or anything else.

Think of buying something covered by your local sales tax. It doesn't matter one wit to the store clerk where you got the money to buy the thing. You will pay a sales tax even if you are buying the item with borrowed funds, as by using a credit card. On the other hand, when you pay off your credit card balance, you don't pay a sales tax again on the repayment. You just reimburse the credit card company for having advanced you the initial sales tax amount, with interest if you pay over time. The Fair Not Flat Tax has just the same effect: the tax consistently falls on spending, however financed. In time we'll come to see why that's a huge improvement over the status quo.

A LITTLE BIT OF HISTORY

I conclude this introduction to tax basics with a quick tour of tax's history over the last century or so. Knowing where we have come from will help us to better understand the mess we're in, and to see a way out.

First Steps

The U.S. income tax began in 1913 after the Sixteenth Amendment to the Constitution gave Congress the power to levy a national income tax. The first income tax was minor: the entire law was only an add-on to a tariff bill and took up just a few pages. Excise taxes (taxes on products such as alcohol and tobacco) and tariffs (taxes on imports) were then the largest source of federal funds, accounting for 90 percent of federal revenue on the eve of World War I. The first income tax's top marginal rate was 7 percent, imposed on only a handful of the wealthiest Americans—less than 1 percent of the population. This original income tax was designed as a progressive tax, one in which the rich pay a higher percent of their income than the not-rich do. Because the tax was so minor, the decision to adopt an income base was uncontroversial. Indeed, much of the support for the movement to get the Sixteenth Amendment ratified in the first place had come from progressive Midwesterners who wanted to force East Coast capitalists and financiers to pay some tax on their wheelings and dealings. Proponents of an income tax were attracted to its theoretical inclusion of savings and the yield to capital. An estate tax was added in 1916, out of much the same spirit.

The Plot Thickens

Things changed for the income tax pretty quickly when America entered World War I. The federal government needed more money, and fast. It looked to its newest tax. Marginal income tax rates shot up to a high of 77 percent on income over $1 million, admittedly a staggering sum in 1918. This was more than enough to get the attention of rich folk, who set to work trying to mitigate or altogether avoid this high burden. The marriage of high tax rates and clever tax avoidance had begun.

Judicial and administrative decisions that seemed logical at first came to haunt the tax later. The most important occurred in 1920, when the U.S. Supreme Court decided that the IRS could not tax the "mere" appreciation of capital assets until they were sold. Little could the justices have predicted that the fateful realization requirement they had thereby created would be the death knell for any hope of a consistent income tax. But the seemingly innocent nontaxation of capital appreciation meant that Congress had to make rules governing "basis" to keep track of that part of an asset's value that had already been taxed. Assets with large built-in gains—appreciation waiting for the appropriate time to be taxed—proliferated.

What a tangled web we were weaving! Various decisions, each sensible in its own way, collided to make for a disastrously porous system. What to do with the built-in gains in an asset when an owner died? Congress decided to ignore them, figuring that the estate tax would take care of taxing wealthy decedents and that it was unfair to tax nonwealthy widows and orphans. Thus originated the stepped-up basis for assets acquired on death, a fixture of the income tax to this day.

All these decisions are straightforward enough. But add together the realization requirement, an income tax's nontaxation of debt, and the stepped-up basis rule, and you get what I call Tax Planning 101: the brutally simple means by which rich property owners can live well tax free. I'll give more detail in the next chapter. Stay tuned.

Meanwhile, the tax cat was out of the bag, on its way to becoming a lion. After dropping a bit after World War I, marginal tax rates rose again under Franklin D. Roosevelt's New Deal. In 1935, also as part of the New Deal, the payroll tax system began. Initially, this was a 1 percent employee tax matched by a 1 percent employer share. It was designed as an actuarially funded system: the dollars paid in would be set aside for an employee's personal benefit. By the end of the 1930s, however, the government needed to infuse cash into the still-stalled economy. Social Security shifted to a pay-as-you-go system. Payroll tax dollars flowed out immediately to current retirees.

The Income Tax Goes Big Time

The income tax was still a small part of the government's revenues until World War II wrought massive changes, brought on by the sudden need for much more tax revenue. The invention of wage withholding enabled the government to collect income and payroll taxes from workers efficiently. Almost overnight, the income tax went from a "class tax to a mass tax," as one scholar of tax history has put it. At the dawn of the war, only a small minority of the rich paid federal income taxes; by the end of it, a vast majority of all Americans did. Marginal rates also shot up, reaching a high of 94 percent at the top bracket, an astonishing figure. After the war rates fell. But not by much. The top marginal rate under the income tax stayed at 90 percent throughout the 1950s.

Since World War II America has had two great tax-cutting presidents. The first was John F. Kennedy, under whose administration the top marginal rate was lowered from 90 percent to 70 percent. It stayed there until Ronald Reagan's administration, when it was brought down to 50 percent in 1981, then briefly to 28 percent in 1986.

The lengthy period of very high marginal rates from World War II to the 1980s, however, did a great deal of damage to the integrity of the income tax. High marginal tax rates encourage aggressive tax avoidance. The underlying mistake of the choice of an income base became more apparent—and more embarrassing. Rates of 70 to 90 percent, falling on work and savings, were disastrously inefficient and seemed grossly unfair to many Americans. At these high levels of tax, the people lobbied hard for relief. The government gave it out freely, and not necessarily for any bad or corrupt reasons. It just didn't seem right to include certain things in a tax base subject to such high rates. A taxpayer in the 90 percent bracket, for example, would have to earn an additional $100,000 to cover $10,000 of unanticipated, nondeductible medical expenses: $90,000 would go to the government, $10,000 to the doctors. To alleviate the hardship, a medical expense deduction was born.

But every time a deduction was allowed or a fringe benefit was excluded from taxable income, all hell broke loose. When we created a deduction for medical expenses, taxpayers retiring in the chilly North argued that they had to move to Florida for "medical reasons." When we allowed nontaxable fringe benefits, workers clamored for them instead of taxable cash. To illustrate, the combination of high tax rates and the tax exclusion of employer-provided medical insurance played a major role in the sorry state of our health care system: it predictably led to a situation in which the well-employed became overinsured while the not-so-well-employed remained uninsured. This is all further proof that tax matters.

Trouble with Capital

Labor and capital are the two major sources of productive value in an economy. If high tax rates and an inconsistent income tax were messy on the labor or wage-earning side, they were disastrous on the capital side. The realization requirement was the hole in the dike. Everyone with money to invest rushed to buy the kind of assets that rise in value without producing cash—who would willingly pay 70 to 90 percent taxes on their yield to savings, when this could be avoided by owning certain assets? The rich then clung to their appreciated assets until death, when the assets could receive a stepped-up basis and their built-in gain would magically disappear. Threatened with a stagnant economy in which no one ever sold anything, Congress had to sweeten the pot. Special lower rates on capital gains were born, typically set at 40 percent of the ordinary income tax rates, to get people to sell assets. (With a top "ordinary" rate of 70 percent, in other words, the capital gains rate was 28 percent, and so on.)

The income tax's theoretical bias against savings also became troublesome to a country that found itself saving too little. The government built more and more exceptions for certain kinds of savings into the tax laws. As all sorts of exceptions to the income tax kept growing, the law got more and more complicated. It was hard for the government even to estimate the effects of the various changes it was making. Tax lawyers and accountants sprang up on every block, advising the wealthy and aggressive on how to exploit the burgeoning loopholes. The officials entrusted with collecting the tax became overmatched—and widely unpopular—because just about every citizen had come to resent the tax.

High wage earners noticed that their property-owning friends were paying a lot less tax than they were. Clever lawyers and accountants used sophisticated tax shelters, complicated devices that allow wage earners to shelter their wages from the tax collector by taking advantage of loopholes normally available only to people with capital. These tax-avoidance techniques became rampant. By the 1980s the government saw that it had to shut down the tax shelter game or it would have no revenue from the income tax at all. Congress attempted to perfect the income tax in the massive Tax Reform Act of 1986. This law lowered tax rates and dramatically curtailed the shelter game, shoring up the income tax's effectiveness when it came to taxing wages. But the 1986 act did nothing about any of the fundamental decisions favoring capital or wealth holders. The rich could still buy, borrow, and die, with impunity.

Tax Today

Meanwhile, a parallel story evolved along much different lines. Ever since World War II the effective yield of the income tax as a percentage of Gross Domestic Product (GDP) has been pretty constant, moving between 8 and 9 percent. The income tax is maxed out. The high tax rates of the 1950s, 1960s, and 1970s led to more exclusions and more avoidance; the lower rates of the 1980s allowed for a broader base with less avoidance. But overall, the bottom line came out about the same. Yet the government grew dramatically in the postwar period. How did it pay for itself? The answer now shouldn't surprise us: the government grew by means of the payroll tax. The payroll tax has steadily gone up until it now collects about 80 percent as much total revenue as the better known, and more despised, income tax. Whereas the income tax as a percent of GDP actually declined a bit from 1945 to 2000, the payroll taxes increased by more than 400 percent.

And so at the dawn of a new millennium, America woke up far from where it started. We have a mess on our hands: an inconsistent income tax that is in effect a wage tax, coupled with an increasingly burdensome payroll tax system. Ordinary workers pay tax on all sides. Clever property owners pay far less or even no tax at all. Rich dads, living tax free off their assets, mock poor dads, who are working to pay the government first, their living expenses second.

The U.S. tax system has become one big, complicated, and unprincipled disaster. Radical plans to scrap it altogether abound. But almost all reform efforts championed by politicians suspiciously and needlessly throw out America's long-standing commitment to at least moderate progressivity in tax, the baby with the bathwater. These flat-tax plans must raise tax rates on the middle class to pay for tax cuts for the rich. What's fair about that, in a world that already overburdens the middle class? As the American people have come to see this, flat-tax fever has waned. But this leaves us with no comprehensive, comprehensible reform plan on the table. The laws that have actually made it through Congress, as well as George W. Bush's major tax-cutting proposal, being considered as I write this, are nothing but ad hoc affairs. They lower rates here, create new deductions or exclusions there. But the fundamental elements of tax persist, even though tax is terribly broken.

It's time to stop trying to patch up a system that was wrongly designed in the first place and that has long since ceased to be consistent or even sensible. America needs and deserves a new tax system, one that is simple, efficient, and fair.

A QUICK LOOK AHEAD

There are several possible variations on the Fair Not Flat Tax, which is simply a consistent, progressive spending tax. My preferred plan features a broad-based spending tax, such as a national sales or value-added tax at a flat rate of 10 percent. (All of my numbers are rough and only illustrative.) It provides a rebate to ensure that the lowest levels of spending bear no net tax. Households that spend more than $80,000 or so on themselves will pay a supplemental personal consumption tax by filling out an annual tax form, which I'll call the Fair Tax form. This personal consumption tax will have rates ranging from 10 to 40 percent, the latter rate falling on households with more than $1 million dollars a year in personal spending. All of this creates a consistent, progressive spending tax at the combined rates in table 1.1.

Table 1.1 Suggested Fair Not Flat Tax Rate Schedule
for a Family of Four

Spending ($)	Tax Rate (%)
0–20,000	0
20,000–80,000	10
80,000–160,000	20
160,000–500,000	30
500,000–1,000,000	40
over 1,000,000	50

The plan would lighten the burden on many lower- and middle-class Americans. Yet it's also a far cry from penalizing rich spenders; after all, the current income tax has rates ranging up to 40 percent. The Fair Not Flat Tax simply levies the tax at a more sensible time than the income tax does, at moderately progressive rates, and with tremendous simplification for most.

T W O

The Trouble with the Income Tax

You must know the difference between an asset and a liability, and buy assets. If you want to be rich, this is all you need to know. It is rule no. 1. It is the only rule. . . . It sure beats saving $100 a month, which actually starts out as $150 because it's after-tax income, for 40 years at 5 percent, and again you're taxed on the 5 percent. That is not too intelligent. It may be safe, but it's not smart.

—Kiyosaki, *Rich Dad, Poor Dad*

THE INCOME TAX AS IT EXISTS TODAY IS A BAD TAX. FEW Americans would argue with that statement. But what exactly is wrong with it? Using only the basic facts about tax discussed in chapter 1, we can now reach a surprising insight. The deepest problems with the income tax relate to its erratic and wrong-headed attempt to tax savings. This leads us to a major theme of this book:

If we stopped trying to tax savings directly, our tax system would get much better overnight.

Once we've come to understand the problems with our inconsistent income tax, we'll also understand the reasons for moving to a consistent spending tax.

Let's back up for a minute. A good tax should be simple, efficient, and fair. That's not asking too much. But the income tax is too complex, too inefficient, and too unfair; it's not a good tax. All three of

27

these problems relate to the basic decision to tax savings directly—
and to our half-hearted embrace of it.

My argument against the income tax in this chapter proceeds on
three tracks. One, America does not have, and never has had, a consistent income tax because we've never taxed all savings. Two, while
in theory one path toward a better tax is to make the income tax
and its commitment to taxing savings more consistent, this is not the
approach America should, or ever will, take. Three, the inconsistent
income tax that we do have is particularly bad because it falls heavily
on the poor dads of the nation while the rich dads delight in their
ability to evade it.

Let's look more closely at the complexity, inefficiency, and unfairness of the income tax.

COMPLEXITY

Because savings are hard to tax, any income tax is bound to be complicated from the start.

If all savings were held in bank accounts that paid simple interest,
taxing savings would be easy enough. Suppose you put $100 in a
bank at the beginning of the year, and the interest rate on the account
is 5 percent. The bank credits your account $5 at the end of the year.
You pay income tax on this amount. The government even tells the
bank to report how much it paid you, just like your employer reports
your wages, so that the IRS doesn't have to rely on your honesty
alone. It's all simple enough.

But bank accounts are not the only way to save. What if you
invest in stocks or mutual funds, or put your money into real estate
instead of in a bank? You might not get paid any interest or dividends
at the end of the year, but your portfolio of investments probably
goes up in value—on average by more than the 5 percent that the
conservative bank account does. If the law consistently taxed savings,
it would have to tax you on the rise in value of your investments
each year, whether that increase was paid out in cash or not.

But the law doesn't do so. Under a legal case decided by the U.S.
Supreme Court in 1920 and never seriously challenged since, the
income tax does not apply to unrealized appreciation. Although the
tax falls on cash dividends paid out by an investment, it does not

fall on an investment's rise in value until there is a sale or some other disposition—a realization event. Thus Rich Dad's Rule No. 1: buy assets. Assets of the right kind don't lead to current taxation.

The Realization Requirement

There are plenty of reasons for the realization requirement. It is hard to value assets before they are sold. People do not always have the cash on hand to pay taxes on unsold assets. An asset that has risen in value one year may go down in value the next. And so on.

Sensible as the realization requirement may be, however, its birth in 1920 marked the death of any consistent income tax. Note that the Haig-Simons definition of income does not entail the realization requirement; income includes all consumption plus all savings, whether the latter is realized or not. Likewise, to an economist or a banker, savings include the increased value of unsold assets, just as savings go down if an asset falls in value. Consider Bill Gates, who owned roughly $50 billion worth of Microsoft stock at the start of 1999, and nearly $100 billion by the end of that (very good) year. Is there any doubt that Gates was worth twice as much by the start of 2000? *Forbes* magazine's editors thought so when they called Gates the richest man in the world and put his net worth at $100 billion, not at some lower figure based on what he paid for the stock years before. (Like many others, Bill lost money in the next year, 2000, but that's how it goes sometimes.)

An income tax with a realization requirement is not an income tax at all. Only *some* savings are taxed: those that reside in the bank accounts that Rich Dad mocks in the opening quotation in this chapter, for example. Other savings, capital investments that appreciate in value—recall Rich Dad's Rule No. 1—are not taxed. *The Millionaire Next Door* and other sources make clear that most wealthy Americans are able to live well by reporting only a small percentage of their net wealth as realized income: the rich enjoy untaxed, unseen, capital appreciation.

The seemingly harmless realization requirement leads to complexity, inefficiency, and unfairness. It generates the most fatal flaw of the so-called income tax: the ability of asset owners to avoid tax while wage earners shoulder an unmitigated load. About three decades ago, the prominent tax scholar William Andrews, one of my professors at Harvard Law School, called the realization requirement the Achilles' heel of the income tax. He was right. The problems have grown worse since then, though the general public has not noticed.

The realization requirement means, among other things, that the law must keep track of the part of your investments that it has already taxed, and the part that it has not. The $100 you put into the bank account my earlier example had already been taxed: it came from money you had left over after you paid taxes on your wages. When you earned the $5 in interest, that got taxed too. So you started the following year with 105 after-tax dollars.

But what if you purchased $100 in stock instead of depositing the money into a bank account? If the stock didn't pay a cash dividend and went up in value by $5, that gain would not be taxed under the realization requirement. For calculating your tax, the IRS needs a way to keep track of the gains that you have not yet paid tax on: the gap between the $105 current value and the $100 original price of the stock. Therein arises the tax concept of basis. *Basis* means, in essence, after-tax dollars. Pay tax and you get basis. Don't pay tax, and you don't get basis.

The problem for tax is that the realization requirement is not just an accounting rule. It gives taxpayers an incentive not to save in simple bank accounts, but to purchase real estate or corporate stock instead. Such investors, like Rich Dad, then accrue a lot of built-in gain, or untaxed appreciation. Built-in gain causes several problems, and lawmakers have come up with various answers to these. When someone gives an investment as a gift, the recipient takes over the donor's basis—what the law refers to as *carryover basis*—and hence takes over the donor's built-in gain. There are complex rules that allow for the nontaxable like-kind exchange of some assets, such as real estate, and rules that allow certain corporate mergers and acquisitions to proceed tax free, with the basis of the corporate stock being preserved. These rules go on and on and on, adding significantly to the law's bulk.

Just as the realization requirement encouraged the nation's wealthy investors to acquire assets, it also discouraged them from ever selling their highly appreciated assets, with their built-in tax time bomb waiting to explode at the time of sale. But this was ineffi-cient, because people wouldn't sell assets to others who valued them more. It was also at least sometimes unfair, because people who had to sell their assets for some reason got hit with large tax bills while those who could go on holding their assets did not. To mitigate the ill effects flowing from the realization requirement, another curious creature was born into the tax laws. Lower tax rates on capital gains came about to reduce the disincentive to sell highly appreciated assets and to prevent the unfairness of some wealth holders paying high taxes in the year of an occasional sale. If and when Rich Dad does sell his highly prized assets, he will now pay tax at a capital gains rate far below what Poor Dad must pay on his wages.

Stepped-Up Basis

The realization requirement makes acute the question of what to do with an asset's built-in gain when a taxpayer dies. One answer, an unpopular one, would be to tax the gain at that time: to make death a realization event. Canada actually does this, and it's been proposed as a change in U.S. law. But all of the problems that led the courts to create the realization requirement in the first place are also present at death: assets are still hard to value, and there may be no cash on hand to pay the tax. It seems harsh to expect the bereaved to have to sell their inheritance in order to pay a tax on it. Although taxation of capital gains on death may become part of the law if and when the death tax dies—this is the subject of chapter 4—it's not going to be a simple or popular provision to enforce.

Another answer to the problem of built-in gain at death is to treat transfers at death like gifts—that is, to have a carryover basis for inherited assets. Heirs would simply take over the decedent's built-in gain and would pay tax only if and when they sold their inheritance. But even the possibility of a carryover basis on death is unpopular: citizens complain that it would be a record-keeping nightmare, for example, because few could figure out the basis that their parents or grandparents had in their assets. Former president Jimmy Carter considered enacting a carryover-basis-on-death rule, but it was a political nightmare; the rule never became law.

The tax law has another answer. It imposes an estate tax on the net wealth of certain decedents' estates, a tax that aims in part to get the rich to pay some tax. Although this so-called death tax is not a very effective or sensible tax, lawmakers considered it a sufficient response to the built-in gain issue. And so they allowed the income tax to ignore built-in gain on death. Cash or property received by bequest is not taxable income to the recipient, and the inherited assets get a stepped-up basis under the income tax for all future purposes. The built-in gain simply disappears in the heirs' hands. The stepped-up basis for assets acquired at the time of death is a key part of Tax Planning 101, a set of basic planning techniques that enables wealthy people to live well tax free.

Tax Planning 101 Revealed

Consider the realization requirement, the stepped-up basis for assets transferred on death, and the fact that borrowing is not income under the Haig-Simons definition. Each rule makes some sense in isolation. Put them all together, however, and you have the end of the income tax. People with money to save and invest can follow a simple three-step plan, one that I teach my tax students on the first day of class:

1. Buy
2. Borrow
3. Die

That's it. By buying appreciating assets and borrowing against the appreciation until death, the fortunate few can have the resources to live the good life tax free. Their heirs can inherit the assets with a stepped-up basis, sell them off, and pay off the debts. Neither the decedents nor their heirs will pay any income tax when using this strategy. They'll avoid the payroll tax by the simple expedient of not working. If the fortunate few play it right and borrow enough— they can even use debt to give money to their children presently— they will leave no sizeable estate on which to pay the death tax either. It's a nice deal.

In the real world there are, of course, some complexities in implementing Tax Planning 101 to the max. But not many. Assets sometimes produce cash dividends, for example, triggering tax, and some individuals are uncomfortable with the high debt and risk levels that Tax Planning 101 might suggest. There are ways to deal with such problems by selectively using margin debt and various forms of annuities, insurance vehicles, financial instruments, and so on.

While going into all the details of sophisticated tax-avoidance plans is not my purpose in this book; rich dads have advisors aplenty. I can, however, clear up one common misunderstanding. You might think that the interest on the debt in step 2 is a cost of Tax Planning 101. But recall the alternative: to sell the assets bought in step 1 and pay tax on the built-in gain. By borrowing instead of selling, one gets to keep the assets. If they rise in value by at least as much as the interest rate on the loan, there is no net cost at all.

Let me be clear about my point here: I am not arguing that everyone who is able to do so takes Tax Planning 101 to its limits, although I can assure you that after years of advising, teaching, and lecturing I have learned that quite a few wealthy people do. Rich Dad seems to have figured it out perfectly well; there is no shortage of clever lawyers, accountants, and financiers giving advice and developing financial plans for the rich. But even if many wealth holders don't take full advantage, the very possibility of Tax Planning 101, in all of its simplicity, ought to give us pause. Any wealthy person—and America is spawning new millionaires by the minute—can avoid paying taxes for the rest of her life. If she does pay tax, it's in some sense a matter of her choice: she pays tax because she wants to keep working, or because she invests in a way that doesn't take Tax Planning 101 to the limit. Tax for the rich is voluntary: they can live perfectly well without it. Not so for the poor and middle class, who must work and pay taxes—first—in order to eat. And therein lies the rub. If we don't do something to change the very possibility of Tax Planning 101, we will never have a consistent or effective income tax for wealth holders.

ARTFUL DODGER

Meet Artful Dodger, a master of Tax Planning 101. Mr. Dodger is fortunate enough to have $1 million at his disposal. It really doesn't matter to us how Dodger came upon his money. Perhaps he inherited it, in which case he would never pay any federal taxes on his good fortune. Or perhaps Dodger earned his stake by working, or he won the lottery, in which cases he has already paid an initial income tax. In any event, now that he has his million dollars, Dodger is through with his days as an ordinary taxpayer. Here is how he manages never to pay taxes again.

Dodger invests his million in a portfolio that gains 10 percent in value every year. In Year 1, Dodger's portfolio rises in value from $1,000,000 to $1,100,000. Dodger borrows $100,000 at 10 percent interest (leaving his net wealth at $1,000,000). In Year 2, he owes $10,000 in interest, but his portfolio has gone up by another 10 percent, or $110,000, so it is now worth $1,210,000. He borrows $110,000 more (leaving his net wealth at $1,000,000). He uses $10,000 to pay off the interest on his Year 1 debt and spends the remaining $100,000. In Year 3, the portfolio again goes up 10 percent, this time $121,000, rising from $1,210,000 to $1,331,000. He borrows $121,000 (again leaving his net wealth at $1,000,000). He uses $10,000 to pay off his Year 1 debt, $11,000 to pay off his Year 2 debt, and spends $100,000.

You get the point. Dodger will always have $100,000 to spend, and his net wealth will always stay at $1,000,000, as long as the interest rate on his debt matches the yield to his portfolio. And if—as one would expect—Dodger is on average earning more on his portfolio than he is paying on his debt, he is actually making money on the deal, too.

The game can go on forever. As long as Dodger plays it, he will pay no income tax, no capital gains tax, no payroll tax, and no gift and estate tax. When he dies, his heirs can use their inheritance with its stepped-up basis to pay off his debt. They will pay no income tax, and Dodger's estate will also have dodged the death tax, which is a tax on one's *net* estate, that is, on assets minus liabilities. Dodger only ever has one million dollars of net wealth, the current exemption level for estate taxes.

INEFFICIENCY

The decision to tax savings led to a series of ill-coordinated decisions that gave rise to the present inconsistent income tax. Under the status quo the rich with property win. Wage earners lose. So should we fix the income tax so that it consistently taxes savings, in whatever form, as they accrue?

I think not. Even over and above its considerable complexities, a consistent income tax would distort individual decision making in a troubling way. The very concept of an income tax is biased against saving and in favor of spending. It is not what America wants or needs.

This wasn't such a big deal when the income tax was established in 1913 as a relatively minor tax on the upper classes. But as the income tax grew—and as both individual Americans and America itself struggled to meet our personal and collective savings needs—the income tax's bias against savings became more and more problematic. This led lawmakers to repeatedly back off of the idea of taxing savings, even beyond the realization requirement. We are left with the fact that some savers, falling under the consistent income tax model, are doubly taxed, while others, exploiting the gaps in the inconsistent income tax model, are not taxed at all. Meanwhile, the law is replete with targeted savings provisions that may not even increase Americans' savings at all.

What does it mean that a consistent income tax doubly taxes savings? This criticism dates back at least as far as the 1848 work of the political and economic theorist John Stuart Mill. I'll consider Mill's double-tax idea with the help of a pair of fabled taxpayers.

The Curious Tale of Ant and Grasshopper

Recall Ant, the thrifty saver who is concerned about the harsh winters ahead. Her counterpart Grasshopper is a spender who lives for the moment. Consider how a consistent income tax would affect them.

Imagine that there is an income tax with a flat rate of 50 percent. Ant and Grasshopper each earns $200 in wages, and so each pays $100 in income taxes right away. Grasshopper immediately spends all of his after-tax money, as is his way, while Ant saves all of hers, as is her way.

If the interest rate on savings is 10 percent, Ant's $100 will grow to $110 by the end of the year. But she will not get to keep the full $110. An income tax views the $10 of interest earnings as additional taxable income. Ant must pay another 50 percent, or $5, on these earnings. This tax on Ant's return to savings is what Mill called the "double" tax. It can be both unfair and inefficient.

Efficiency requires that the government stay out of private decisions. In a world without taxes, it wouldn't matter to the government whether a citizen spent or saved. The interest rate sets the appropriate return to savings. Irving Fisher, a great economist in the early part of the twentieth century, called interest rates the price of impatience—what people need to be paid not to spend now. In a world without taxes, one could spend everything now, like Grasshopper, or have savings plus the interest it earns, like Ant. The market would take care of getting things right by raising the interest rate just enough to attract the total amount of savings that society wants and needs.

In a world with an income tax, however, the government mucks things up. The tax actively prefers spenders over savers. Money put into immediate consumption is taxed once and only once. No matter how long Grasshopper enjoys whatever he does with the $100 he has left after taxes, he will never be taxed on it again. But for Ant, both the initial savings *and* her reward for not spending it immediately are taxed. This is especially harsh when much or all of the return to savings is merely compensation for inflation, as the accompanying story of "Inflationary Blues" illustrates. Because of the second tax on savings, all else being equal, people will save less under an income tax than they will under a consumption tax. Tax cigarettes and fewer people will smoke; tax savings and fewer people will save.

INFLATIONARY BLUES

Suppose that inflation were running at 10 percent. Ant's $100 at the start of Year 1 would be worth—or would be the same thing as—$110 at the start of Year 2. This is what inflation means: under a 10 percent general increase in prices, it will cost Ant $110 to buy exactly the same winter coat Grasshopper bought a year earlier for $100. But because of the second tax on her $10 of earnings, Ant will not have $110. She will only have $105, and she won't be able to afford the coat. This situation suggests another principle:

When interest rates only compensate for inflation, ordinary savers lose value over time under an income tax.

The problem of taxing gains that merely compensate for changing monetary values has led to arguments that we should index the basis of investment assets for inflation. That may be a good idea in terms of efficiency and fairness, but it would further add to the complexity of the income tax. This is just one more way that the very attempt to tax savings is doomed to be complicated, inefficient, and unfair from the start.

Economists debate the actual bottom-line effects of an income tax's bias against savings, however, in part because economists debate everything. Yet there is a real-world puzzle. Facing a tax on savings, some people might save *more*. These are people saving to build up a nest egg. Because their savings bear a tax, they need to save enough to have their nest egg *and* pay this tax; they will have to save more than they otherwise would.

It is challenging to quantify all this, and impossible to be precise, given the complexities of observing real-world behaviors. But it is also not necessary to be precise. Most economists agree that a consumption tax is more efficient than an income tax. If we could turn back time and start over again with a consistent consumption tax, we would be a wealthier, happier people today.

The Virtues of Saving

Because saving is a good activity both individually and collectively, taxing it is inefficient from both an individual and a collective point of view. On an individual level, there are plenty of good reasons to save: for retirement, to provide for emergencies, to buy a house, to put a child through college, and so on. Yet common sense, experience, and expert studies all suggest that most people have a hard time saving for anything. We are shortsighted, like Grasshopper. Many of us will come to rue the days we didn't save more. This is one of the reasons why the Social Security system was established: to help us save for retirement, because many of us won't do so on our own.

Today the inconsistent income tax is full of provisions granting favorable tax treatment for pension plans, IRAs, and other targeted savings vehicles, such as the Clinton-era medical savings accounts. Trouble is, these laws are simply incoherent under the present inconsistent income tax. Recall Tax Planning 101 and the income tax's noninclusion of debt. What's to stop a taxpayer from putting money into an IRA with one hand while borrowing with the other, thus getting a deduction with no net saving? Still, the mere existence of these pro-savings provisions tells us a great deal about the values and activities America wants to promote. Yet all this just leads to an obvious question with no obvious answer: If many social policies are designed to encourage people to save more in their own best interest, why should the principal federal tax system be set up to *punish* saving?

Saving is also good on the collective level. Having money available for investment is a good thing for the economy: the more capital there is, the lower interest rates become. Lower interest rates help us all, as politicians found out when the economy boomed after we began to cut down our national debt in the 1990s. The beneficiaries of increased saving include, importantly, workers, because lower in-terest rates encourage more investment in labor-saving technology and leave more social product available to be paid out in wages. Lower interest rates also help consumers, who can pay less for their home mortgages and credit card debts, and students, who will not have to pay as much interest on their student loans.

A concern with capital is not illiberal or conservative. Jesse Jack-son—no right-wing supply-sider—once remarked that without cap-ital, capitalism is just another "ism." It's unfortunate that few liber-als have been so logical. When the Fair Not Flat Tax is fully on stage before us, I will show how a consistent, progressive consumption tax, by encouraging the rich to save, not spend, can move America to a promising model of class teamwork, not class conflict.

A high savings rate and corresponding lower interest rates also en-courage long-term planning. They help us to provide a better world for our children and our children's children. It is, of course, possible for a country to oversave, as John Maynard Keynes helped to teach us when we were in the depths of the Great Depression, but America is far from having *that* problem today. Almost all economists agree that we could do better by saving more. (And if under a consistent consumption tax we ever did start to save too much, the right answer would be to cut the consumption tax's rates so as to lower the price of present spending, not to reverse course and again try to tax savings directly.) So once again we face an obvious question with no obvious answer. If having more savings is in our national interest, why should the principal federal tax system be set up to *punish* savings?

BATTLE OF THE BEST-SELLERS

In case you can't get too excited about ants and grasshoppers—notwithstanding the popularity of *A Bug's Life*, the animated film that starred the two legendary insects in their thrifty and spend-thrift roles—we can also consider two sets of protagonists drawn from late 1990s best-sellers.

In *The Millionaire Next Door*, Thomas Stanley and William Danko present a real-life portrait of the typical American million-aire, drawn from many surveys, interviews, and focus groups. The authors discovered that the average millionaire is a hard-working, high-saving, frugal man or woman—a perfect ant. In *Die Broke*, Stephen Pollan and Mark Levine consider the high tax toll shoul-dered by those who would pass on wealth to their children at death. Pollan and Levine offer advice on how to enjoy wealth while alive and "die broke"—how to be a perfect grasshopper, that is.

This caricature is somewhat unfair to Pollan and Levine's fine book, which presents numerous sound financial tips given the cur-rent state of the law. But die-brokers and millionaires next door are exemplars of major themes in this book. A problem with cur-rent tax policy is that it punishes millionaires next door, even though they are among our best and most productive economic citizens. At the same time, today's tax law encourages the wealthy to become die-brokers, even though such advice, if widely followed, would hurt us all. In short, today's tax law is backward in relation to prototypical American lifestyles and values.

UNFAIRNESS

An income tax is complex, which helps to explain why America has never had a consistent income tax. Even if we could adopt a perfectly consistent income tax, it would be inefficient, especially at a time when we need more—not less—savings. Still, there's one goal left to consider before we leave the income tax behind: fairness. After all, neither simplicity nor efficiency is all that there is to life. The simplest and most efficient tax system imaginable is a head tax—one that simply collects a flat dollar amount from every man, woman, and child. Yet few would seriously consider a head tax, where Bill Gates would pay the same dollar amount in taxes as a fast-food worker, to be fair. The quest for fairness moves us to consider more complex, particularized taxes that adjust tax burdens to reflect our different economic stations in life.

Indeed, I believe that fairness is the most important element of a good tax system; that's why I wrote this book. If fairness dictated that we directly tax savings, we could retain and possibly even try to perfect the income tax, living with some complexity and inefficiency as we did so. But is it really fair to tax savings? There are two recurring—and stubborn—arguments that it is.

One, only the rich save to a large extent. Those of us who are not rich consume a high percentage of our income—approaching 100 percent or even more for those who live off of credit cards. Some people therefore argue that a consumption tax is regressive: the poor and middle classes will pay a higher percentage of their income in tax, because the savings of the upper classes won't be taxed at all. But this argument ignores the attractive possibility of a *progressive* consumption tax like the Fair Not Flat Tax. It also, like many theoretical arguments, ignores the practical reality of the current inconsistent income tax, including the fact that the rich can consume tax free today under Tax Planning 101. We shall come to see that the Fair Not Flat Tax is a very effective indirect tax on capital, simply levied at the time that wealth is cashed out for personal spending. It's much better at getting at Rich Dad's ways than the status quo is; it shuts down Tax Planning 101.

Two, some people contend that a fair tax should reflect a taxpayer's ability to pay. Because both savings and the return to savings are resources available to a taxpayer, these people believe that both should count in determining that ability. To illustrate, Ant has ten dollars more at the end of a year of savings than she and Grasshopper started with, so it is right and proper, this logic goes, to expect her to share more with the rest of us in the form of taxes. Once again, this argument sits poorly in light of the status quo. The forms of savings most consistently taxed under today's inconsistent income tax are precisely those most likely to be used by the lower classes: simple bank accounts. These poor ants get double taxed and lose real value against inflation. Meantime, the wealthy flock to pension plans and the super wealthy to Tax Planning 101—they are happy grasshoppers with plenty of ability, but no obligation, to pay tax on their high-spending ways.

Let me be perfectly clear: I agree with "ability to pay" as a general principle informing the fairness of any tax. But the fatal flaw of even a consistent income tax is that it determines one's ability to pay at the wrong time—at the time of earning from labor or capital, rather than at the time of spending. The Fair Not Flat Tax will get at the rich—but when, and only when, they show their ability to pay by choosing to spend money on themselves.

SOME FINAL THOUGHTS ON THE INCOME TAX

Before moving on to consider alternatives to an income tax, I want to underscore four related points, for I know from experience that arguments for old taxes, even bad old taxes, die hard.

One, for most Americans there is no real difference between an income tax and a consumption tax, because most Americans don't save. Recall the Haig-Simons definition: Income = Consumption + Savings. If Savings equal zero, then Income = Consumption. This is life for those of us who live paycheck to paycheck.

For the most part, then, the difference between an income and a consumption tax base directly impacts only the wealthy. But this does not mean that the choice of tax is unimportant. Far from it. Savings matter. The attempt to tax savings has had major consequences for tax policy in America. What the rich do with their money is important for the rest of us mainly because it is important to our national economy. Saving is good for us all. We ought to be encouraging the rich to save; it is exactly the same thing as encouraging them not to consume so much on themselves. We also ought to be making it easier for ordinary working-class people to get into the savings habit. Any true income tax is backward in this regard.

Two, the argument for a consistent consumption tax such as the Fair Not Flat Tax is not an argument about the proper level of national savings. It is not a narrowly empirical or supply-side argument about the virtues of savings per se. It is true that a consistent income tax falls on work and savings and thus relatively discourages them. A consistent consumption tax falls on spending and thus does not necessarily discourage work and savings. Yet we don't know that for sure. Economists debate whether there will actually be more work and savings under a consumption tax. A consumption tax makes it easier to save, so some people might work and save less because they don't need to work and save as much to make ends meet. The net effects are difficult to quantify.

But the argument against an income tax and for a consumption tax like the Fair Not Flat Tax does not depend on any precise measurement of actual effects. It is not an argument like the supply-side supporters of Ronald Reagan and other conservative Republicans might make. I am not saying, let alone promising, that there will be X percent more work or Y percent more savings, or that GDP will increase by Z percent under a consumption tax. Washington, D.C., today is overrun with economists working in plush think tanks, cranking out "dynamic analysis" to show how much richer we would all be if we could just cut taxes their way. Most of this stuff is nothing more than "voodoo economics," as the elder George Bush called it two decades ago. I am not relying on witchcraft. The argument for the Fair Not Flat Tax is about simplicity, efficiency, consistency, and—first and foremost—fairness. It rests on an appeal to our enlightened common sense. It is not about the total size of the nation's capital stock. Under a consistent consumption tax, if we saved too much—and thus consumed too little—the right remedy would be simply to lower tax rates.

LUXURY FEVER

In his recent book, *Luxury Fever: Why Money Fails to Satisfy in an Era of Excess*, psychologically oriented economist Robert Frank describes contemporary American spending habits and compares these with data on what really makes people happy. Frank argues that much of our spending on luxuries is part of a no-win process. We are drawn to spend more and more to compete with our neighbors and maintain our station in life. Such spending doesn't truly add to happiness. It's just a rat-race. Frank argues that an increase in personal savings, especially among the affluent, would be good for us individually and collectively.

Luxury Fever concludes with a strong argument for a progressive consumption tax quite similar to the Fair Not Flat Tax. Frank adds the interesting argument that such a tax would make even rich spenders happy by helping to break the vicious cycle of their luxurious lifestyles. Even without showing that we would be doing rich spenders a favor, however, there are many compelling reasons to adopt a progressive consumption tax—one that would reduce luxury fever and help add to our nation's pool of savings.

Three, moving toward a consistent consumption tax does not mean that the law will abandon a liberal commitment to getting the rich to pay their fair share. Abandoning the income tax may appear to be an inherently conservative move. But it is not.

First off, the argument that the income tax is more progressive than any consumption tax rests on the assumption that we consistently tax savings. But America doesn't consistently tax savings, and it doesn't really want to tax savings. We have backed off from a consistent income tax model. We just haven't done so systematically enough, and therein lies one major rub. Second, the argument for taxing the rich more than the rest of us is best left to a discussion of the appropriate tax *rates.* If we want the rich to pay more on average than the not-rich, we can do this by imposing higher rates on them. For now we are trying to figure out *what* to tax, and I hope you have come to see that income is not an attractive base. But the base of the tax has nothing at all to do with *how much* we tax it. For it is a fact that

Consumption taxes need not be flat taxes.

Four, and finally, moving to a consistent consumption tax does not mean that the law will oppose consumption, which many people consider to be the "engine of our economy." Indeed, the Fair Not Flat Tax is more pro-consumption—and more genuinely progressive—than the mess we're in. The Fair Not Flat Tax simply chooses to impose the inevitable taxes of modern life on spending rather than on work or savings. It retains progressivity by imposing higher rates on higher levels of spending. In fact, a good reason to implement the Fair Not Flat Tax is that it will achieve more equality, more fairness in consumption—it will make it a little bit easier for the lower and middle classes to consume, in part by making it harder for the rich to consume and getting them to save more instead.

The Fair Not Flat Tax expects the fortunate few to share more with the rest of us because they are in a position to live so well themselves. Anyone who can afford to spend more than a million dollars a year on personal pleasures can also afford to share more with the rest of us than an ordinary consumer does. The Fair Not Flat Tax aims to reverse the current pattern of rich dads and poor dads whereby the rich asset holders get richer while the poor workers get poorer. That pattern is not fair. It should change. Under the Fair Not Flat Tax, it will.

THREE

The Case for a Spending Tax

As never before, the U.S. income tax system is under attack. Almost no one seems satisfied with the way it works, complaining that it is overly complex, unfair, and inhibits economic growth. In spite of this widespread dissatisfaction, what exactly should be done about it commands much less agreement.

—Joel Slemrod and Jon Bakija, *Taxing Ourselves: A Citizen's Guide to the Great Debate over Tax Reform*

WE HAVE SEEN THAT A CONSISTENT INCOME TAX IS A BAD idea in theory. Further, an inconsistent income tax is a horrible reality. We should drop the foolish attempt to tax savings directly, and adopt a consistent consumption tax.

We are almost ready to grasp the argument for moving to a quite particular alternative, a consistent, progressive, postpaid consumption, or spending, tax. But on the way to recommending this Fair Not Flat Tax, I will add a final—and hopefully clinching—argument to the general case for consumption taxes: They're what everybody seems to want.

This is hardly obvious at first. Anyone listening to the calls for tax reform in postmillennial America might think that they are all just so much noise. Everybody hates the income tax. Almost everybody hates the IRS. But beyond these obvious truths, it is hard to say much about what the public thinks. Everyone seems to have a more or less realistic plan for fixing the mess we're in. Politicians call for a flat tax, national retail sales tax, value-added tax, USA Tax, any sort of tax but what we now have. It seems impossible to find a common theme amid the madness of the crowd.

But there is indeed such a common theme. Knowing only what we've learned in the first two chapters, we can look about us and see something quite surprising:

> **All of the calls for major tax reform today**
> **are calls for a consumption tax.**

This is a remarkable bit of news, all the more so because few journalists, politicians, scholars, and other Americans seem to have figured it out. In this chapter I'll explore various trends in talk of tax with this theme in mind. Let's begin by going back to the not-so-distant past to help us see the way to a better future.

THE NOBLE FAILURE OF
THE TAX REFORM ACT OF 1986

Calls for tax reform have not always been calls for a consumption tax. In the 1980s, a decade of significant tax reform, policymakers such as Senators Bob Packwood, a Republican, and Bill Bradley, a Democrat, saw two distinct options for getting us out of the mess of the inconsistent income tax. Both options were laid out in an important 1977 U.S. Treasury Department study, *Blueprints for Tax Reform.* On one hand, we could give up the income tax altogether and go the route of the Fair Not Flat Tax—a consistent, progressive consumption tax. This was the road not taken. On the other hand, we could attempt to perfect the income tax, to render it more consistent. That's what we tried.

Recall that as the 1980s began, the income tax was trapped in a vicious cycle. The top marginal rate in 1980, when Ronald Reagan was elected president, was 70 percent. Under such high rates, claims for deductions, credits, and exclusions—both legal and questionable—came pouring in. The more the loopholes widened, the smaller the tax base became, and the higher rates had to become on what was being taxed in order to meet the government's revenue needs. Tax shelters that allowed wage earners like Poor Dad to take advantage of Tax Planning 101–style loopholes became rampant. The tax system was losing its integrity and its efficacy and was teetering on the brink of disaster.

Senators Packwood and Bradley and others saw the mess. They concluded that a consumption tax was unfair because it did not tax savings. Here again, the fatal flaw in income tax supporters' logic became apparent: they failed to see that to tax savings directly was unwise in theory and unrealistic in practice and that a progressive spending tax could indirectly get at capital much more fairly and effectively than an inconsistent income tax ever could. In any event, the bipartisan strategy reflected in the Tax Reform Act of 1986 was to fix the income tax: to significantly broaden the tax base by removing scores of deductions and tax preferences so as to reduce marginal tax rates. The act shut down the most popular tax shelters, raised the standard deduction and personal exemption levels (to get people off the income tax rolls), eliminated many deductions and credits, and repealed the capital gains preference. Marginal tax rates fell all the way to 28 percent for the highest earners. It seemed as though the income tax was made whole, at long last.

Two *Wall Street Journal* writers, Jeffrey Birnbaum and Alan Murray, celebrated the Tax Reform Act of 1986 in a popular book, *Showdown at Gucci Gulf: Lawmakers, Lobbyists, and the Unlikely Triumph of Tax Reform.* ("Gucci Gulf" refers to a corridor in the Capitol where well-heeled lobbyists hang out, looking to angle for tax breaks for their clients.) *Gucci Gulf* painted a heroic picture of bipartisan lawmaking overcoming all obstacles, including inertia, complexity, and greed, to improve the tax system.

The celebration was premature. Barely a decade after the Tax Reform Act of 1986, the top marginal rate had risen to 39.6 percent— well below its historic highs, but also well above the 28 percent where the 1986 act had left it. A preferential capital gains rate—particularly for savings—was back. New deductions, credits, and exclusions had sprung up, along with a new generation of tax shelters. The income tax was as inconsistent as ever.

With the benefit of hindsight, we can see that the Tax Reform Act of 1986 was a well-intentioned but ultimately doomed quest. The framers of the act were trying to perfect the income tax, but they did nothing about any of the basic steps in Tax Planning 101. They failed to touch the realization requirement. They didn't change the income tax's treatment of debt. They didn't alter the rule about stepped-up basis on death. To people with wealth, "buy, borrow, die" remained sound—and brutally simple—advice. What the Tax Reform Act of 1986 did—and did very effectively—was to shore up the status of the income tax as a *wage* tax by making it harder to hide labor earnings from the tax collector. But with Tax Planning 101 left intact, property owners like Rich Dad could keep sleeping soundly, free from tax worries.

The Tax Reform Act of 1986 ought to go down as the high-water mark of the attempt to have a working income tax in this country. Indeed, Congress went as far as is it is likely ever to go in that direction. It just didn't go far enough, and it failed. Ever since 1986, all major comprehensive tax reform proposals have been for some type of a consumption tax.

COMPREHENSIVE REFORM SINCE 1986

After the bipartisan moment celebrated in *Gucci Gulf*, tax politics reverted to business as usual, with typical partisan divides. Republicans sponsored a host of radical tax reform plans in the 1990s while Democrats were content to try to hold down the fort. Democrats argued with Republicans about the appropriate tax base: Democrats supporting the income tax, Republicans opposing it. Ditto for the gift and estate, or death, tax. Republicans took the lead in ushering forth bold new plans—to abolish the IRS, to repeal the entire tax code, to shift to a flat tax, sales tax, value-added tax, and so forth. Democrats such as Bill Clinton, meanwhile, proposed ad hoc, incremental reform of the status quo. In short, Democrats fiddled while Republicans burned.

But on closer examination we discover that even the Democratic fiddling had a distinct theme. Although a few Democrats would move tax back in the direction of a consistent income tax—Representative Dick Gephardt of Missouri, for example, proposed an income-oriented reform, a "flat" tax plan with four rate brackets (no truth in labeling there) that would include most forms of savings in the tax base—much of the Democratic tax agenda involved consumption-oriented changes. This is easy to miss because Democratic proposals were couched in the language of protecting the income tax against the barbarians at the gate.

Consider several prominent aspects of Bill Clinton's tax policy. There were no radical new tax laws under Clinton's presidency like the Economic Recovery Tax Act (ERTA) of 1981 or the Tax Reform Act of 1986 under Reagan's. Aside from a $500-per-child credit and an expansion in the earned-income tax credit for the working poor, almost all of the changes under Clinton were steps in the direction of a consumption tax. The highest tax rate on capital gains was reduced from 28 percent to 20 percent. This was not the zero-percent rate of the contemporary flat-tax plans that I'll consider shortly, but it was clearly a step in that direction. Another Clinton-era change greatly expanded the exclusion of gains from the sale of personal homes. Investment in a home is an important form of savings; the nontaxation of most of the appreciation in personal residences was significant consumption tax treatment. Further changes in the 1990s expanded IRAs and added tax-favored savings vehicles to help parents provide for their children's education. Once again, this is consumption tax treatment. During the 2000 presidential campaign Al Gore, following his leader, called for more of the same: a series of ad hoc, targeted credits, many featuring consumption tax treatment of savings plans.

Now let me be clear again: helping parents save for their children's education, workers save for retirement, and many taxpayers become homeowners are noble enough goals. The problem is the fundamental inconsistency in the Democratic approach to tax policy. The uneasy mixture of consumption and income tax elements has made for an inconsistent income tax riddled with loopholes. By retaining a supposed income tax structure while continually adding more consumption tax elements to it, well-meaning Democrats do no lasting good for the cause of principle in tax. Tax Planning 101 remains unchecked. Taxpayers like the rich and clever Artful Dodger can pay no tax at all under the ineffective parts of the income tax while taxpayers like the thrifty Ant continue to incur a double tax under the remaining effective parts.

A DEAL WITH THE DEVIL?

Several years ago Congress began what may become a disturbing trend. It created so-called Roth IRAs. Unlike traditional IRAs, these new devices give no tax deduction up front, but also unlike traditional IRAs, they do not tax withdrawals from the accounts (provided certain requirements are met, of course).

In other words, Roth IRAs are funded with after-tax dollars, but the return on the savings is then tax free. Like traditional IRAs, they follow a single-tax, consumption model. But because their single tax occurs up front, Roth IRAs are prepaid consumption taxes, akin to wage taxes.

As a matter of personal financial planning, the decision to go Roth or traditional is straightforward: when do you expect your marginal tax rate to be higher, when you put money into an account or when you withdraw it? Many workers currently in the 15 percent income tax bracket might well figure that they are likely to be in a higher bracket later in their lives. For them, a Roth IRA makes good sense.

There are now bills to expand Roth treatment to even more pension plans. There is something disturbing about this. Without addressing the fundamental incoherence of the inconsistent income tax, it isn't clear how much if any new savings Roth plans will generate. Worse, these plans are steps in the direction of prepaid consumption taxation, making the system look more and more like a wage tax—the wrong kind of consumption tax from a fairness perspective. Why then is Congress so enamored of Roth-style savings inducements? The answer isn't hard to come by. Because Roth-style plans collect taxes now and forswear them later, present members of Congress prefer them to postpaid consumption tax models, where the tax is collected on someone else's watch. To politicians who like to spend money today, what's the good in a tax due tomorrow?

If only Democrats could see the light! A consistent consumption tax—the Fair Not Flat Tax—would help parents, retirees, and homeowners by *never* taxing savings. It would bring consistency at last, simplifying the entire tax system and making it more principled and fair. And it would get rich people who finance a high-end lifestyle with capital to bear *some* tax, as they should but now don't. This would in turn lower the burden on ordinary workers. All of this could be gained by understanding what it is they are doing anyway. For even though it is fundamentally flawed, the hesitant and halting Democratic approach to tax policy furthers this chapter's principal theme:

Most of the recent reforms to the income tax have been steps in the direction of a consumption tax.

FLATLAND

More radical—and coherent—consumption tax ideas have come from the Republican side of the political aisle. Among the most popular and persistent calls for tax reform in the 1980s and 1990s were those for a flat tax. Robert Hall and Alvin Rabushka's 1985 treatise, *Flat Tax, Simple Tax, Fair Tax,* was especially influential in shaping this movement. It helped to inspire the lower, flatter rate structure of the Tax Reform Act of 1986. In a sign of the times, Hall and Rabushka published a second edition of their book—now titled more simply *The Flat Tax*—in 1995, amid another outbreak of flat-tax fever. Many politicians, such as the presidential candidates Steve Forbes and Jack Kemp, signed on.

A flat tax sounds attractive because of its rate structure. "Simpler, flatter, fairer" is the mantra of the flat-tax crowd. Whether *flat* really means "simple," however, is not clear. Little of the complexity of the current tax system comes directly from its progressive rate structure. Many of the simplifications advocated by flat-tax proponents come instead from adjustments to the tax base—basically eliminating the attempt to tax savings directly—that can be made under any set of rates. Whether *flat* really means "fair" is even more debatable. I'll take up that thorny issue in chapter 5. There is, however, little doubt that Americans don't like high tax rates, and *flat* sounds low.

But this, like so much of the popular rhetoric about tax, ain't necessarily so. Most Americans—the working classes, yet again— would have to pay more under a flat-rate tax than they would under even a moderately progressive tax. A progressive tax at least at-

Table 3.1 A Typical Flat-Tax Rate Schedule

Earnings ($)	Tax Rate ($)
0–20,000	0
over 20,000	20

tempts to get the rich to pay more than the average American, and therefore it can keep tax rates down for the lower- and middle-income classes. As the working folk came to see this, the initial ardor for a flat tax cooled considerably, and the tax's fairness claims were called into question. It is no coincidence that the Republican candidates who won their party's presidential nomination, both Bushes and Bob Dole, called for lower but not flat tax rates.

But there was more to the flat-tax plans than met the eye. We don't have to wait until chapter 5 to see that two central features of all of the major flat-tax plans were not about flat tax rates at all. First of all, the common plans were not flat-rate plans. They all featured *two* rates, the first being a large zero bracket. Typical plans would allow approximately $20,000 for a family of four to go tax free, after which a tax rate of around 20 percent would kick in. The plans would look like what you see in table 3.1.

It might seem a quibble to call this a two-rate plan. But the rate structure of the popularly proposed flat taxes is interesting as a concession to fairness. Proponents of the typical flat-tax plans accepted the idea that low levels of the tax's base (whether that base is wages, spending, or income) should not be taxed. By including a zero bracket, the flat-tax plans deviate from any simple, "neutral" principle that every dollar should bear an equal rate of tax. They thereby opened the door to many more questions about the appropriate rate structure. If a family's first $20,000 of consumption should not be taxed at all because this money is likely spent on life's necessities, for example, why can't we say that a wealthy family's last $10,000 of consumption should bear a somewhat higher rate of tax because this money is likely spent on life's luxuries?

Second, the proposed flat-tax plans all featured a consumption base. They invariably contained a zero rate of tax on capital gains, interest, and dividends. That is, they exempted the yield to savings from the income tax's "double" tax. Recall from Ant's example in chapter 1 that a consumption tax could be pre- or postpaid, and prepaid consumption taxes are wage taxes. The common flat-tax plans were all wage taxes.

Let's take a moment to see this point in a different light. We know from both the Haig-Simons definition and common sense that all money is either spent (consumed) or not spent (saved). Consider where that money can come from—what the sources of the inflows are. There are three basic ones:

- work, in the form of wages
- the return on savings, in the form of interest, dividends, or capital gains from the sale of assets
- gifts and inheritances

No serious tax or tax reform proposal in America would tax the recipient of gifts and bequests. (The so-called death tax falls on donors, not recipients, as I'll discuss in the next chapter.) The inconsistent income tax does not. The flat-tax plans follow suit. Because flat-tax plans also systematically exempt the return on savings, they are left to tax only wages. Once again, the flat-tax plans are wage taxes. Money is taxed up front, when earned, and never again. The return to savings goes tax free. Hall and Rabushka are direct about this point; in *The Flat Tax* they refer to their proposal at various times as a wage tax. We can conclude the following:

The flat-tax plans are equivalent to a wage tax like the Social Security tax.

Now we can see what's wrong with flat taxes, from a fairness point of view. Any popular flat-tax plan would simply add another wage tax to the payroll tax system, accentuating the problem at the core of American life: the excessive struggles of the working class compared to the excessive luxuries of the moneyed class.

NATIONAL RETAIL SALES TAX

Another characteristically Republican idea is to replace the inconsistent income tax with a national retail sales tax. A national sales tax

Table 3.2 National Sales Tax with Rebate

Spending ($)	Tax Rate ($)
0–20,000	0
over 20,000	20

has considerable appeal. It sounds even simpler than the flat tax, and it fits perfectly well into our present theme. For:

A sales tax is a form of postpaid consumption tax.

Under a sales tax, money is taxed when it is spent; there is no double tax on savings, as there is with a consistent income tax. Sales taxes follow the simple rearrangement of the Haig-Simons definition, Consumption = Income − Savings. Because they ignore savings until they are cashed out, sales taxes are consistent spending taxes.

Like the flat-tax plans, leading national sales tax proposals accommodate the lowest levels of consumption. A typical plan does so by mailing everyone—or sometimes just the lowest wage earners—a rebate. For example, if there were a 20 percent national sales tax, every person might receive a rebate of up to $1,000 on a showing of at least $5,000 in earnings. A family of four that earned at least $20,000 combined could get $4,000 back. The sales tax together with the rebate would mean that this family would pay no net tax on its first $20,000 of consumption: the 20 percent sales tax on this spending would generate $4,000 in taxes, but the rebate would exactly offset this amount. We'll see later that cash rebates can play an important role in simplifying the Fair Not Flat Tax plan. For now, note that the practical effect of such rebates is exactly the same as that of having a $20,000 zero bracket (see table 3.2).

And so the sales tax with a rebate has exactly the same effect as the flat tax with its zero bracket; the difference between the two plans is that a sales tax is a postpaid consumption tax and a flat tax is a prepaid one. But given that each has the same single rate, the sales tax and the flat tax will result in exactly the same tax, as Ant's example in chapter 1 helped to teach us.

VALUE-ADDED TAX

There are practical reasons to worry about a large-scale national sales tax. Cheating can be prevalent under such a tax, for example: merchants might just pocket the tax and not mail it in. Next there is the political temptation to exempt lots of items, such as food and medicines, although the rebate provides a better mechanism for accommodating the necessities of life. Reaching out to include items of personal consumption that come from services would be difficult, yet services are a large share of the national economy. The higher the sales tax rate, the greater these problems become. Many scholars believe that while a 5 to 10 percent national sales tax might be feasible, a 15 to 20 percent one is unlikely to be. For this reason, most countries that have implemented either a sales tax or a value-added tax (VAT) have chosen the latter. There is increasing talk around America of adopting a VAT as a partial or complete replacement for the inconsistent income tax, notwithstanding the people's suspicions of this foreign-sounding device.

For the central theme of this chapter, the key point is that the tax base of a VAT is identical to that of a sales tax:

A value-added tax, or VAT, is a form of postpaid consumption tax, like a sales tax.

A TALE OF A TEAPOT

Consider the simple case of a silver teapot with a VAT in place.

Al goes into a mine and collects silver ore that he sells to Betty for $1. Under a 20 percent VAT, Al pays a tax of 20¢ on his dollar.

Betty refines the ore and makes it into silver, which she sells to Carl for $5. Betty then determines her profit: $5 in gross receipts minus the $1 cost of the ore. She pays 20 percent of the $4 profit, or 80¢.

Carl works the silver into a teapot and sells it to Donna, a retailer, for $10. Carl pays a VAT on his $5 profit, adding $1 to the government's till.

Donna finally sells the finished teapot to Ethan, a customer, for $20. Donna then pays the 20 percent on her profit of $10, for a tax of $2.

> Note what has happened by the time this chain of events has reached its conclusion: the various parties have collectively paid a 20 percent tax on the $20 teapot. A total of $4 (.20 + .80 + 1.00 + 2.00) has gone to the government. The bottom line is exactly the same as it would have been if a 20 percent sales tax had been imposed on the final buyer, Ethan. Instead of Ethan paying the 20 percent tax on the twenty-dollar price of the teapot, Al, Betty, Carl, and Donna each paid a 20 percent tax on the value added to the teapot at his or her stage of the process. Together they paid 20 percent on $20, or $4.

The idea of a VAT is to collect the flat consumption tax gradually on the manufacturing and production side of the consumer market rather than all at once on the retail end. Each firm in a chain of production pays a VAT on the value it adds to the process. The firm takes its gross receipts, subtracts the cost of its inputs, and pays tax on the difference. (There is a difference between this subtraction method VAT, the form most commonly proposed in the United States, and a credit invoice VAT, the form most commonly employed around the world. Under the latter, a company pays tax on its gross receipts and then gets a credit for taxes paid by its suppliers.) Because the value-added tax is collected gradually, it doesn't depend on the honesty of retailers alone. Instead, the government can rely on various willing informants: each time a firm subtracts the cost of its purchases, it effectively reports to the government some other business's receipts.

You might be thinking that a major difference between a sales tax and a VAT lies in who pays it. In the case of a sales tax, the buyer pays; in the case of a VAT, various manufacturers and sellers do. But this is a distinction in form only; there is no bottom-line economic difference. A VAT is a cost of doing business, like payments for salaries or supplies. Firms must factor the VAT into their prices. Who ultimately bears the burden of the tax depends on complex market factors of supply and demand, but it will certainly not be manufacturers alone. If you doubt that, consider this: You don't really pay the sales tax as a buyer; sellers do. They are the ones legally responsible for sending the money in to the government. But the next time you buy something for one dollar and are told it will be $1.10 "with the tax," try telling the store clerk that *he's* responsible for the sales tax, not you. Sellers simply raise the price of the goods they sell so that the tax money comes out of buyers' pockets. Adam Smith once noted that in the end all consumption taxes are paid by the buyer. Exactly the same thing ought to be true in the case of a VAT.

VATs and sales taxes have the same tax base; they are both flat-rate, postpaid consumption taxes. And so our theme persists.

INDIVIDUAL CONSUMPTION TAX: THE USA TAX

There's one more comprehensive tax reform proposal to consider. In 1995, then Senators Sam Nunn, a Democrat, and Pete Domenici, a Republican, following the recommendations of an extensive blue-ribbon commission, introduced a tax plan known as the USA Tax. *USA* stands for "unlimited savings allowances." Of the options we've looked at so far in this chapter, the USA Tax most closely follows the form of the equation Consumption = Income − Savings.

The USA Tax would be administered in much the same way as what we know as the income tax. It features tax forms just like the dreaded 1040s. Basically, you add up all of your income, then sub-tract all contributions to the unlimited savings accounts. It's exactly as if there were no limits on tax-deductible contributions to IRAs under the current income tax. As with IRAs, withdrawals from USAs would be taxable.

We know, of course, that such a tax is consumption based. It does not tax money put into savings. It is a postpaid consumption, or spending, tax, like a sales tax, because it taxes only money that is spent. But unlike the single-rate sales tax plans, the USA Tax main-tains a progressive tax rate schedule. Rather than paying taxes at the point of purchase, taxpayers fill out annual returns that, through the logic of the Haig-Simons definition, reflect their spending for the year. (And note how much easier it is to pick up such items as the purchase of personal services, the cost of which remains when we subtract savings from income.) Proponents called the USA Tax an

"individual consumption tax" to note its similarities to the "individual income tax" that most Americans think we have now. But in
keeping with our running vocabulary:

> **The USA Tax is intended to be a postpaid consumption, or spending,**
> **tax, identical in its base to a sales tax. In theory, the only difference**
> **between the two taxes lies in the rate structure—the sales tax**
> **is flat, the USA Tax is not.**

GETTING CLOSE

The USA Tax has two attributes that we should want in a broad-
based tax: it is progressive and it falls on spending, not on work or
savings directly. The plan also has a distinguished intellectual lin-
eage. The idea was developed by the eminent British economist Nicholas Kaldor in the mid-1950s. It was advanced and applied to an
American context by the Harvard Law Professor William Andrews
in the early 1970s. Later in the 1970s, David Bradford, then a mem-
ber of President Ford's Treasury Department and now an economist
at Princeton and New York Universities, used the progressive consumption tax as the model for the government study later published
as *Blueprints for Tax Reform.* You will recall that *Blueprints* suggested two avenues for solving America's tax troubles. The USA Tax
was the road not taken.

The USA Tax plan gets close to the mechanics of the Fair Not Flat
Tax. It is a progressive spending tax. But the USA Tax, so attractive
in theory, has its flaws in practice. It is not, in fact, a *consistent*
spending tax; it shares some of the vices of the inconsistent income
tax. For one thing, the USA Tax supplements its consumption base
with an estate tax; it is thus a progressive consumption-plus-estate
tax. But as we shall see more fully in chapter 4, an estate tax isn't
needed under a consistent spending tax: dead men don't spend. The
Fair Not Flat Tax, on the other hand, is a progressive consumption-
without-estate tax.

More important, the USA Tax is inconsistent in its treatment of
debt because it fails to include the proceeds of borrowing as income.
The treatment of debt is critical to an effective tax: borrowing is a
form of negative savings or dissaving. A tax built up on the idea of

subtracting savings from income (C = I − S) must *add* negative savings, or borrowing, into its base. A postpaid consumption, or spending, tax that doesn't tax borrowed money spent in personal consumption leads to inconsistent results. In practical terms, a taxpayer could get a deduction for contributions made into a USA on one hand, consume out of borrowed money with the other—and pay no tax. It sounds hard to tax debt used to spend, but note that the far simpler sales tax has it right on this score: debt used to consume should be taxed, repayments of debt should not be. This is how a sales tax works. A progressive spending tax that doesn't tax the proceeds of debt used to finance consumption is an inconsistent consumption tax. But on the big questions in tax, we need consistency.

A BETTER WAY

This brief tour of comprehensive tax reform options has brought us to the threshold of a better way. We began where we are now in America: with an inconsistent income tax perched precariously between a consistent income tax that would include all savings in its base and a consistent consumption tax that would include none. Today's tax has elements of both a prepaid consumption (wage) tax and a postpaid consumption (spending) tax. In the end, the inconsistent income tax taxes wages effectively and taxes capital ineffectively. The Social Security payroll tax piles on top of the inconsistent income tax to further the burden on ordinary wage earners. The entire mishmash of tax has left us in the worst of all possible worlds. Tax today thwarts Poor Dad's attempt to escape from his paycheck-to-paycheck lifestyle and allows Rich Dad to live a life of leisure, free of tax.

The inconsistencies of tax breed complexity, inefficiency, and inequity. The Tax Reform Act of 1986 was a logical, comprehensive reform that tried to perfect the income tax model. But the act failed to go after the heart of the problem—the structural features that make Tax Planning 101 an effective tax-avoidance strategy for the rich. After the dust had settled, it became evident that the 1986 act had merely shored up the income tax's status as a glorified—and hideously complex—wage tax, leaving property owners like Artful Dodger more or less untouched. In hindsight, the failure was inevitable. America lacks both the will and the way to have a truly consistent income tax. In and of itself, this isn't a problem: an income tax isn't necessarily a good tax, as chapter 2 showed. But we should wake up to that reality and stop trying to make the income tax work.

The 1986 act's failure left the field free for consumption tax proposals. In they came. First came the flat tax, a prepaid consumption or wage tax. It is sensible not to directly tax savings. But a flat rate structure would abandon America's long-standing commitment to at least moderate progressivity in tax. It would raise taxes on the middle classes to pay for tax reductions for the rich. And the flat tax levies its single tax at the wrong time—at the moment of work, not spending. Combined with payroll taxes, the flat-tax plans would give us a regressive wage tax system, leaving Rich Dad alone.

The proposed national retail sales tax and the more or less equivalent VAT were improvements. These taxes are consistent, postpaid consumption (spending) taxes. Consistent spending taxes apply to spending however it is financed, whether out of current labor earnings, savings, someone else's wealth (that is, gifts or bequests), or debt. Tax Planning 101 no longer works as a means of escaping tax because Artful Dodger must pay a tax when he borrows and spends. A spending tax also falls consistently over a taxpayer's lifetime, based on her choice of lifestyle, as we saw in chapter 1.

So sales taxes and VATs get the base, or the *what*, part of tax down right. They tax only spending, including spending financed by debt. But these tax plans needlessly give up on any attempt to achieve a progressive rate structure. While the common proposals for flat spending taxes make some accommodation for the lowest levels of earnings or spending, they don't differentiate any more than that: John and Jane Doe pay the same tax rate on their middle-class lifestyles as Bill Gates and other multibillionaires pay on their luxurious ones. Tax increases on the middle classes finance tax reductions for the rich. Added to the federal payroll tax, the whole system looks regressive. I do not believe that flat is a fair answer, as I will argue more fully in chapter 5.

The USA Tax almost got us to the promised land. Like sales taxes or VATs, it is a postpaid consumption, or spending, tax. Unlike its simpler relatives, it maintains progressive rates. But the fatal flaw of the USA Tax lies in its inconsistency: it maintains a separate estate tax, and it fails to include consumption paid for by debt. The USA

Tax thus fails to shut down Tax Planning 101. Artful Dodger and friends would still be able to buy, borrow, and die, tax free.

The Fair Not Flat Tax is the logical next step. It's a consistent, progressive spending tax. It's thus the right answer to America's ailing tax system, in practice as in theory.

We're almost ready for the concrete details of how the Fair Not Flat Tax works. But first, we need to consider two more issues: why a consistent spending tax needs no separate death tax, and why a fair tax ought not be a flat one.

FOUR

Death to Death Taxes

Inheritance is a terribly inefficient way to pass wealth to others. Estate taxes are among the highest the IRS levies, ranging up to 55 percent, depending on size. Then there's state tax. And if the estate is primarily in a qualified retirement plan—not an uncommon occurrence—the bite can even soar as high as 70 to 85 percent.

—Stephen M. Pollan and Mark Levine, *Die Broke*

THE FINAL PIECE OF THE TAX-BASE PUZZLE CONCERNS gifts and inheritances. Current law taxes these to the donors under a distinct federal tax—the gift and estate tax. This tax serves as a companion to the income tax, which never has included gifts or inheritances within its definition of taxable income. Congress, following George W. Bush's lead, voted to repeal the tax as I wrote this book, but the repeal won't go into effect until 2010, and no one but a fool would bet that Congress won't change its collective mind before then.

A major cloud over the repeal lingers because of continued partisan politics over the issue. Conservatives call the gift and estate tax the "death tax" and adamantly support the repeal. Although I don't consider myself a conservative, my own work has been influential in this regard: in 1994 I wrote an article for the *Yale Law Journal* that the *New York Times* credited with beginning the anti–death tax movement. Liberals, in contrast, just as adamantly oppose radical reform. They advocate instead various partial, ad hoc moves, such

as lessening death tax rates, building in special provisions for owners of farms and family businesses, and raising the tax's exemption
level.

It's time to stop the bickering, because this is an issue on which
all can agree—if only they would listen. What we have learned so
far about tax leads us to a conclusion that will no doubt still surprise
many:

**There is no need for a gift and estate tax under a consistent
postpaid consumption tax.**

The lesson of this book so far is that we should tax spending,
not work or savings. Dead people don't spend. Hence there are very
compelling, principled—and perfectly bipartisan—reasons why we
shouldn't have death taxes. The Fair Not Flat Tax eliminates both
the inconsistent income tax and the ineffective gift and estate tax,
substituting a single, consistent, progressive spending tax for both
taxes. Personal spending becomes the sole tax base. That's the fair
thing to do.

THE NATURE OF THE BEAST

Let's back up and consider some facts about the gift and estate tax.
America has had an estate tax of some form since 1916, three years
after the modern personal income tax was put in place. To close up
one obvious loophole—the ability to give everything away on one's
deathbed—Congress added a gift tax in 1932. Both taxes fall on the
donor, not the recipient. The gift and estate taxes have since been
unified into a single tax system that I will refer to as the estate, or
death, tax for short.

Most Americans never have to worry about the estate tax. Only
1 to 2 percent of people who die in this country each year leave
enough wealth behind to generate any estate tax at all. The tax con-
tributes only about 1 percent of all federal revenues. For people rich
enough to be concerned about it, however, the estate tax can be a
steep tax indeed. It starts in at a rate of 37 percent and quickly reaches
a flat 55 percent. A small percentage of taxable estates pay a large
percentage of the total estate taxes collected.

Legal Loopholes

These high tax rates are accompanied by large loopholes, creating more trouble in River City. Three major exceptions to the estate tax eat away at its effectiveness.

One, gifts or bequests left to a spouse are typically not taxable because of the marital deduction. There are numerous complexities in this accommodation for spouses, nearly all of them unfortunate, but the bottom line is that most married couples do not pay an estate tax until both of them have died.

Two, each person has a lifetime exemption level of about $1 million before any tax is due—this is the zero bracket of the estate tax. The unified credit amount, as the exemption level is called, was $600,000 in 1981. Congress decided to raise it to $1 million over a period of years from 1997 to 2006, but later decided to get to the $1 million level by 2002 and raise it further, to $3.5 million, thereafter. Each person can give away this $1 million, cumulatively, in life or at death without incurring any tax. A husband and wife, with careful planning, can combine their lifetime exemption amounts so that a married couple can leave $2 million to their children tax free.

Three, in addition to this $1 million per person benefit, there is an annual exclusion amount of $10,000 per donor per donee. Once again a husband and wife can combine their amounts. A married couple can give $20,000 to each of their children each year without incurring any tax or subtracting from their lifetime exemption amounts. This is exactly what books like *Die Broke* recommend, as in the opening quotation for this chapter. Inheritance is indeed "a terribly inefficient way to pass wealth to others." But this doesn't mean that one shouldn't pass on wealth in some other manner. There's more than one way to skin a cat.

How It All Works

The basic operation of the estate tax is easy to explain. When a person dies, the IRS adds up all of the assets in her estate at their current fair market value. It next adds in the value of any taxable gifts she made during her life—that is, gifts that exceeded the annual exclusion amounts. Finally, the government subtracts debts. If all of that comes up to less than $1 million—as it does for the vast majority of American decedents—there are no further questions. If the decedent's estate is worth more than $1 million, the government next subtracts any qualified transfers to a surviving spouse. Then and only then is the estate tax paid, at the steep rates noted above.

Many other special provisions relate to such things as charitable contributions; payments for tuition and medical expenses; trusts; ownership of farms and small, family-held businesses; life insurance; and so on. The estate tax system is enormously complicated. It finances legions of well-paid estate tax lawyers and planners. But you know enough now to grasp what is basically wrong with the death tax and to understand the best option for fixing it: outright repeal in the context of comprehensive tax reform.

The Best-Laid Plans: Why We Have an Estate Tax

Before getting to the arguments against the estate tax, let's consider the case for it. There is little doubt that the tax arose out of noble motives, in the midst of a wave of progressive thought in America. It was designed to help break up large concentrations of wealth and to make sure that heirs would not get too large a head start in life: the tax aimed to level the proverbial playing field. Some tax theorists today still consider the estate tax an important backstop to the income tax because, as we well know by now, the latter fails to capture much of the yield to savings during a wealthy taxpayer's lifetime. The estate tax is meant to correct this oversight.

Support for death taxes has deep roots. The eminent nineteenth-century political theorist Jeremy Bentham thought that an inheritance tax was the best of all possible taxes. John Stuart Mill, who had criticized the income tax's double tax on savings, concurred. Because an estate-type tax would be collected from the dead, Bentham and Mill reasoned, it wouldn't interfere with any important incentives to work or save. Further, because under English and American law no one has a right to an inheritance, the tax also wouldn't interfere with anyone's sense of entitlement. It seemed like a win-win situation—a tax without burden. But Bentham and Mill were thinking about moderate tax rates—a 10 percent tax in Mill's case—and they had a primitive idea of the psychology of the rich. Times have changed.

THE CASE AGAINST DEATH TAXES

Just as with the income tax and its inconsistent commitment to taxing savings, nearly a century of experience with the estate tax has
proven it to be a failure. The tax is porous and complex. It might
even be counterproductive, costing the government money simply
to have it in place. This is because the tax has a long-term effect on
the incentives to work and save and because it encourages transactions—like complicated life insurance trusts—that cost the government income tax revenue. These costs may well outweigh the limited
benefits of the tax.

The estate tax is also failing to achieve its non-revenue-related
goals. The concentration of wealth in America has gotten more, not
less, uneven in the decades since the tax was put in place. To those
few who are fluent in the language of tax, this isn't surprising. Tax
Planning 101 combines with Estate Planning 101, which we'll all
learn in a moment, to allow vast sums of wealth to cross generational
divides, and then enables the heirs to live perfectly well without paying any taxes throughout their privileged lives.

Perhaps most striking of all, given that it is a tax on the wealthiest
minority, the estate tax is not popular. Polls consistently show that
most people are opposed to death taxes. California overwhelmingly
voted to repeal its version of a death tax in 1982, and many other
states have followed suit. Canada, Australia, and Israel—each a
Western-style democracy—have repealed their death taxes. A tax
that runs contrary to common-sense morality is difficult to maintain.

Like its historic sibling, the income tax, the estate tax has severe
practical problems. Valuing assets and liabilities without market
transactions is difficult, for one thing. Death is an awkward time to
be trying to do so, for another. High tax rates generate incentives
to explore any and all tax-avoidance options. Intrafamily transfers
are extremely hard to monitor. Clever, well-paid estate tax planners
exploit the numerous tensions, ambiguities, and loopholes in the law.
This leads to costly, complicated forms of ownership that are difficult
to police. And the obviously deep-seated desire to pass on wealth to
one's heirs means that policymakers who try to reform the estate
tax, to plug its loopholes, constantly face an uphill struggle.

Loopholes of questionable legitimacy pose problems aplenty. But as with the inconsistent income tax, even the perfectly legitimate exceptions—in this case, the annual exclusion and lifetime exemption amounts—are significant enough to bring the estate tax's very being into question. Because its provisions create incentives to give large amounts of wealth away early in life, the estate tax in practice doesn't serve one of its principal intended functions, to level the playing field, just as the inconsistent income tax fails to serve one of its principal original goals, to tax the yield to capital. Artful Dodger manipulates tensions within the inconsistent income tax, using Tax Planning 101 to avoid paying taxes altogether. So too can asset holders take advantage of the rules of the estate tax to make sizeable transfers of wealth without paying a penny of tax.

The Same Old Story

The trouble with the income tax springs from two basic causes. One, its attempt to tax savings directly is complex, inefficient, and unfair, leading to an inconsistent income tax in practice. Two, even a consistent income tax comes due at a poor time. The tax falls on earnings regardless of whether the money is spent or saved; ordinary citizens who must labor both for present and future needs are hit hard.

The estate tax suffers from the same two problems. It, too, attempts to tax savings directly: the unspent wealth left over at the end of a saver's life. But savings are hard to tax in life or at death, and so any attempt to tax them is bound to be complicated. Taxing savings also pushes people not to save in the first place, or to engage in intricate manipulations to avoid taxation, both of which are inefficient things to do. Worst of all, the estate tax is unfair, because it penalizes the thrifty and ignores the spendthrift; it taxes savers, not spenders. And if work and savings are unwise and unfair triggers for tax, death is a horrible one.

None of this means that we should let heirs, or anyone else, off the hook. Far from it. But there are better times to tax than at the grave site. The Fair Not Flat Tax consistently taxes spending, at progressive rates, regardless of how the wealth is obtained or whether the spenders are first or later generation rich folk.

Estate Planning 101

It is a mistake to think that tax avoidance strategies are only for the narrowly selfish, rich people who want to spend all that they can on themselves alone. It is, of course, true that the easiest way to avoid the estate tax is to spend it all now and die broke. But many wealthy individuals do not want to spend every last penny on themselves, as *The Millionaire Next Door* and abundant real-world experience suggest. By taking advantage of basic planning techniques using the annual exclusion and exemption amounts, however, the rich can pass tremendous amounts of wealth—altogether tax free—on to later generations. If they lack cash because they are holding onto capital assets to play Tax Planning 101, they can either gift away these assets in sophisticated estate-planning strategies or, more simply, just borrow money to give to the kids.

The basics of estate tax avoidance, like the basics of income tax avoidance for those with property, are brutally simple:

1. **Give early**
2. **Give often**
3. **Give in trust**

The fortunate heirs on the receiving end of such tax-savvy wealth transfers will find themselves in a perfect position to play Tax Planning 101: they'll have property, the indispensable ingredient for living a tax-free life. The nastiness of taxation need never sully their privileged lives. To make matters even easier, professional trustees can do all the work of avoiding taxes for them. A simple example illustrates the point.

The Lears: A Tragedy of Tax Policy

As in Shakespeare's play, King Lear has three daughters, Regan, Goneril, and Cordelia. The Lears are wealthy and well advised. Every year they give each daughter the full $20,000 that the law allows them to give tax free. It's not a difficult matter to put this money into trusts so that the daughters cannot spend it imprudently.

Over time, these gifts can become a large sum of money indeed. Invested in the stock market at a historic 10 percent rate of return, each daughter's trust with its annual $20,000 will grow to over $1 million by the time she reaches age twenty, over $3 million by age thirty, and nearly $9 million by age forty. Once each daughter marries, the elder Lears can include the son-in-law in the wealth-transfer extravaganza by doubling their annual gift to $40,000 per year to each daughter's household. The Lears can extend the game further as grandchildren are born. All of the later Lears can play Tax Planning 101 with their wealth, so they need never pay any income, payroll, or any other kind of tax. Nor need they ever work a day in their lives.

It can get worse. Suppose that the Lears had decided to endow one of their daughters with their full exemption amount, $2 million, at the time of her birth. (Within a few years, if the law doesn't change, this figure will be $7 million—strongly suggesting that increased estate-tax exemption levels, without more, aren't the path to tax fairness.) Very wealthy Americans can easily afford to do just this. When that endowment is supplemented with the $20,000 annual gifts, the lucky Lear will have a personal fortune of almost $100 million by her fortieth birthday! If she plays the full Artful Dodger game, she can live happily ever after at a spending level of $10 million a year—all without ever paying a penny to her distant Uncle Sam.

The current income-plus-estate tax with all of its loopholes and flaws—a tax that is built up and defended in the name of fairness—allows and even encourages this sort of thing. It's a travesty, at least, if not a tragedy.

A TALE OF THREE DAUGHTERS

Not only is the current estate tax so porous as to call its claims of fairness into question, but also when it does fall, it falls on the wrong parties. Recall the tale of Ant and Grasshopper. An income tax treats thrifty Ant worse than spendthrift Grasshopper. Consider now the divergent fates of the Lear daughters in terms of the lives they lead and the taxes they pay.

Suppose that King Lear has cleverly taken advantage of the annual exclusion amounts to build up a trust for each of his daughters. As each turns twenty-one, Lear presents her with a completely tax-free gift of $1 million. From this equal starting point, the three children go off in different directions down life's paths.

Regan, the eldest daughter, spends all of her money nearly at once, partying and carrying on. She must then beg her parents for more. But at least she avoids paying any tax on her large initial stake or the pleasure it brought.

Goneril lives more prudently. She hires a skilled investment advisor to play Tax Planning 101 for her. This advisor plans a steady annual stream of payments for Goneril, so she can enjoy her wealth while alive, and then die broke. With this strategy she can spend something like $100,000 a year for life, tax free. As a single woman, Goneril lives comfortably on this. In fact, her personal spending is at the same level as that of someone who has worked hard and earned $200,000 a year in wages but has seen half of these earnings taken away in a combination of federal, state, and local income and payroll taxes, along with the many other expenses of the working world. When Goneril later marries, the family lives on her husband's income while Goneril's "trust money," as she calls it, continues to subsidize her personal spending habits. Goneril outlives her husband and spends all of her inheritance from him too. When she dies, broke, her three children inherit nothing.

In this scenario Goneril, like her sister Regan, never pays any federal taxes—no income, no payroll, no gift or estate taxes. Indeed, she never works for pay or saves anything in her life; instead, she engages in a steady pattern of dissaving her father's and her husband's money.

Cordelia, the youngest daughter, follows a different route. She puts her $1 million into an investment account, prudently managed in stock funds. She vows to withdraw capital only if she needs to— if an emergency should befall her or if she needs the money to help care for her beloved father in his old age. Meanwhile, Cordelia continues her education and gets a job that pays a decent salary of perhaps $60,000 a year. On these earnings Cordelia pays something like $20,000 in various taxes every year and lives comfortably on the remaining $40,000, or $3,333 a month.

Then Cordelia marries—reasonably well, as they say. She, her husband, and their three children never do withdraw any money from "Grandpa's gift," as the family takes to calling it. By the time Cordelia dies at the age of eighty-four, the Lear legacy, invested in stocks at that 10 percent rate of return, has grown to over $500 million. But if Cordelia tries to pass this on to her children and grand-children so they can live as she did, the government (unless it really has killed the death tax) will take away over half of the wealth in taxes.

Cordelia, alone among the three daughters, will have paid tax—and quite a bit of it, at that. She alone among the Lear daughters contributed work, taxes, and capital to the common pool of social resources as she lived. In reward for her thrift, she alone among the Lear daughters had to contemplate a further and most onerous tax as she lay dying.

ROSS'S WORLD

Fact is at least as strange as the fictional tale of the Lears. Even short of the kind of confiscatory rates that some liberals have urged, the present estate tax—when it is paid—is bad news. Consider H. Ross Perot, with his personal fortune of $3 billion or so. What tax rate does Perot face on additional work? If Ross earns another dollar, the income tax will take about 40 percent of it. He will be left with 60 cents. That 60 cents will become part of his estate and will ultimately be cut down again by the 55 percent estate tax. That tax will take another 33 cents, leaving only 27 cents of the initial dollar. Wealthy taxpayers like Perot, Ted Turner, and Bill Gates thus face tax rates of 73 percent and higher on their additional work efforts. They might as well spend their money running for high-ranking elected offices—as Perot did in 1992. He used $60 million of his money to run for president, thereby saving over $30 million in eventual estate taxes.

There is something odd about this. All three daughters were equal as of their twenty-first birthday. The major difference between them is that Cordelia chose to work and save throughout her life, while her elder sisters chose to spend. The tax collector added another difference: Cordelia alone had to pay taxes, in life and at death. Why should the frugal and thrifty among the rich be taxed—and heavily—at their deathbeds, while the spendthrifts who live luxuriously are not?

HONEST ABE'S WAY

Abraham Lincoln was a notoriously frugal man who spent most of his life in poverty. But he also worked hard to do well by his wife and family. By the time he was a few years into his presidency, Lincoln had managed to become a somewhat wealthy man who could anticipate a comfortable retirement. Yet he continued to be frugal, even to the point of becoming angry at his wife for one of the few times in his life when she bought new furnishings for the White House. Honest Abe thought it an outrage that his house should have new things while Union soldiers had no blankets. When Lincoln died, aides found several months of uncashed presidential paychecks in his desk.

People like Lincoln who die with wealth have done three good things for society. One, most of them have worked hard rather than living the life of leisure that their wealth might allow. Two, they have saved, contributing to the common pool of capital that helps everyone—by keeping interest rates low, for example. Three, they have not spent all of their wealth on themselves: they have not lived a life of pure luxury that would set a dubious example for their friends and family. These savers have gone the route of the noble Cordelia, not that of her prodigal elder sisters.

CORDELIA GETS SMART

You may not be shedding a tear for Cordelia; after all, she has $500 million in an investment account as she lays dying. You might even think—as do long-time advocates of death taxation—that it is fair and just to break up this large concentration of wealth. But before you become too wedded to your conclusions, think again.

Cordelia is unlikely to die with $500 million in her own name. The very existence of the death tax is likely to motivate her either to spend it all on herself and possibly stop working—to be more like her sisters, that is—or to play Estate Planning 101 and give the wealth to her kids earlier, more often, and in trust. Suppose that by the time she was thirty, Cordelia had three children of her own and started giving them $20,000 a year each, completely tax free. This pattern of giving would knock more than $100 million out of her estate. If she also used her and her husband's $2 (or $7) million in exemptions to give to the kids at the same time, that would take more than another $200 million (or $1 billion!) out of her estate as she lay dying at age eighty-four. Add on in-laws, grandchildren—and a dash of the truly sophisticated estate planning I'm ignoring here—and Cordelia could easily avoid paying any estate taxes: the full $500 million would have disappeared from Uncle Sam's grasp. All of this wealth would have flowed down to later generations so that they could play Tax Planning 101 and never pay any taxes in their lives. And so it goes.

THE FATAL FLAW OF DYING BROKE

In *Die Broke*, Stephen Pollan and Mark Levine recommend that wealthy persons use up all their wealth while alive to avoid passing it on to their heirs at death. In large part, this recommendation follows from two facts related to the well-intentioned but wrong-headed estate tax. One, the tax itself takes away up to 55 percent of what one tries to pass on, so leaving a bequest is foolish and inefficient. Two, the expectation or fact of receiving a large inheritance can make heirs unmotivated, lazy, and unproductive. The tax system plays a role in this phenomenon, too. After all, current tax policy encourages the early-in-life transmission of wealth, so heirs like Regan and Goneril get their inheritance when they are young. If we repealed the gift and estate tax, parents could pass on their wealth when they die—and when their children are typically in their fifties or sixties, having already established their lifetime habits. Current tax policy also leaves the heirs alone once they have received their wealth, so it gives them no incentive or structure to be prudent or thrifty—indeed, the estate tax counsels just the opposite, to spend now and die broke. A consistent progressive consumption tax such as the Fair Not Flat Tax, in contrast, would penalize self-indulgent spending among second and later generations of wealth holders.

We ought to be concerned about a die-broke philosophy and about a tax system that encourages it. If too many people followed suit, our national pool of capital would dry up, large amounts of wealth would be passed to young people not best suited to handle it, and our wealthiest senior citizens would be going on lavish spending binges. This hardly seems like the best of all possible worlds to be encouraging.

The Fair Not Flat Tax—a postpaid consumption-without-estate tax—best reverses the travesty of the Lear stories. It does so by eliminating the Lear daughters' perverse incentives to spend or give away all their money, and it makes sure that the Lear heirs pay some tax sometime—when and as they spend.

Things are not always what they appear to be in tax, which is why careful analytic thinking is needed. All of the goals of estate tax proponents—breaking up large concentrations of wealth, leveling the playing field, getting heirs to pay some tax—are best met in a consumption tax system without an estate tax. As part of getting tax right, it's time to listen to logic and public opinion, and to abandon too-long-standing liberal dogma.

THE MILLIONAIRES NEXT DOOR, OR WHY PEOPLE SAVE

Early advocates of estate taxes such as John Stuart Mill thought that such taxes were good because they wouldn't interfere with incentives to work or save. Economists then implicitly adhered to what we now call the life-cycle theory of savings. They believed that people saved money during their peak earning years only to even out cash flow during their own lifetimes. Because most of us make almost all of our money during a limited period of time—from our twenties to our sixties, say—we need to save during our high-earning years to pay off the debts of our youth and to finance our retirement. If people really did save only for life-cycle reasons, any money left over at the end of their lives would be, in a sense, a mistake—it would be there only because the savers couldn't predict exactly when they would die. An estate tax wouldn't change decisions made during one's lifetime at all. The government would simply benefit from taxpayers' errors in calculating the time of their deaths.

Like a good deal of the theory supporting the estate tax, the life-cycle theory of savings behavior turns out to be wrong in practice. People who save do not do so merely to provide for themselves during their own lifetimes. Life-cycle savings follow a die-broke mindset. But most wealthy people in America are millionaire-next-door types. They are not generally people who care only about themselves, who look to spend every last penny on their narrowly selfish desires. They care about their children and their children's children. When they save, they do so for a combination of reasons. They want to provide a pot of money for emergencies, for their own and their family's possible future needs. Millionaires next door care about their financial independence. If they are fortunate in life's games, they may even make more money than they feel comfortable spending on themselves—they simply would rather save than spend at some point, so many keep saving as a matter of habit. Millionaires next door are frugal. They might plan to dip into their savings on a rainy day, but if the storm never comes and they end up with something left over, they have a third motive for saving. They look forward to passing their good fortune to their families, perhaps just as their parents had left them something. Many rich people anticipate giving all or part of their wealth away to charities. Millionaires next door are altruistic. They don't look forward, by and large, to dying broke.

The estate tax runs against this order of things. It puts a crimp in the natural urge to pass on wealth within our families. This is why so many wealthy people use complicated forms of trusts to avoid the estate tax's sting. It is also why a large majority of Americans, rich and poor, disapprove of death taxes.

A SEMANTIC NOTE

Some tax theorists argue that under a consumption tax donors should pay taxes on gifts or bequests because these represent "consumption." After all, benefactors get some pleasure out of giving, or why else would they do it? And if they get joy out of it, giving must be "consumption." As far as words go this argument is fine. But sensible tax reform should not be a matter of words. Lots of things bring joy to us, including contemplating a fine sunset, but it would be silly to try to tax all of them. Gifts and bequests are different from other forms of consumption because they preserve capital in a common store of value. A typical state or local sales tax wouldn't apply to gifts or bequests of assets any more than it would to the consumption benefits of viewing a sunset. So too the Fair Not Flat Tax need not tax transfers of capital.

If a benefactor buys a thing and gives it away, a consistent spending tax like the Fair Not Flat Tax will tax her; in that case we would say that consumption took place at the giver's level. But when the same benefactor passes on cash or investment assets, this is another matter. The gift alone need not trigger tax, because the savings still persist: there has been no final, personal spending of financial resources. The Fair Not Flat Tax allows savings to build up and be transferred tax free. In this way it encourages long-term savings, which are good for the economy. It taxes spending on personal items, whoever does the spending, whenever it occurs. Because heirs, and not dead people, spend, the Fair Not Flat Tax taxes the heirs when they spend. It's all perfectly sensible—and directly opposite to what we do today.

SEEING SOME LIGHT

Finally, I address four points to liberal readers in particular. I know from experience that many of you don't get the argument against the estate tax. You see that such a tax falls only on the rich, and at exactly the moment these fortunate few try to pass on their wealth to a second or third generation. You support the estate tax because you think that it breaks up concentrations of wealth and prevents heirs from gaining an unearned advantage.

Please think again.

One, the actual estate tax fails to do what you want it to do. It doesn't keep wealth out of the hands of subsequent generations. In fact, it can do just the opposite—it prompts many people to give to their children early, often, and in trust. The stories of the Lear daughters illustrate what happens today. The estate tax has so many loopholes in it that it encourages exactly the kind of second-generation wealth accumulation that it was designed to prevent. And a weakened estate tax is worse than no tax at all, for it preserves only the illusion of progressivity. Consider again the Lear examples, now with a $3.5 million per person exemption level.

Two, opinion polls tell us that the average citizen simply doesn't agree with your liberal infatuation with death taxes. It isn't wise for tax policy to fly too often, too far, in the face of common sense. The people can be wrong, of course, but they are entitled to be heard.

Let's try to respond to public opinion by determining whether we can develop a fair tax—one that reasonably well checks the power and influence of the very rich—without resorting to death taxes. It turns out that we can do just that with the Fair Not Flat Tax.

Three, many liberals have a tendency to demonize the wealthy, and a further tendency to lump together all members of any demonized group. To many liberals who subscribe to the soak-the-rich philosophy, all people who oppose the estate tax are just plain "selfish," as Bill Clinton's Secretary of the Treasury, former Harvard University economist (and now Harvard's president) Larry Summers, called them. Summers later had to retract his words in the face of widespread protest, but many liberals silently agreed with him. But what exactly is selfish about the behavior of the many millionaires next door, who work hard and save well all their lives? The Fair Not Flat Tax aims to bring common-sense morality into the tax system. It tries to get away from a traditional class-confrontation mindset and into one of class teamwork instead. By working and saving, the thrifty rich help us all. Let's let them do so.

Four, and finally, not all rich people are the same. Some are hard-working, high saving, and thrifty. Others flaunt their wealth by living the luxurious life. How can the government possibly sort out the two types? It turns out that it can do so easily—by getting the tax system right. Our current system with its inconsistent income and porous estate taxes spares spenders and scorns savers. By any sensible light that's backward. The Fair Not Flat Tax does just the opposite, and it stays away from the grave site in the process. Let's hope more liberals can see the light of its sensible ways.

FIVE

Progressivity Can Live

It is this idea of Robin Hood, or taking from the rich to give to the poor, that has caused the most pain for the poor and the middle class. The reason the middle class is so heavily taxed is because of the Robin Hood ideal. The real reality is that the rich are not taxed. It's the middle class who pays for the poor, especially the educated upper-income middle class.

—Kiyosaki, *Rich Dad, Poor Dad*

UNLIKE THE COMMON FLAT-TAX PLANS THAT WOULD raise taxes for the middle class in order to lower them for the rich, the Fair Not Flat Tax affirms America's historic commitment to a moderately progressive rate structure. Before I defend more fully the "Not Flat" part of the Fair Not Flat Tax, it helps to get some basic facts and vocabulary straight.

THE TERMINOLOGY OF TAX RATES

People often get confused about tax rates. This is easy enough to do with a complex tax like the income tax. Because this tax relies on varying rate brackets, it involves two distinct kinds of rates. One, a marginal rate, is the rate a taxpayer pays on her next dollar of income: if she is in the 33 percent tax bracket, she pays thirty-three cents in tax on the next dollar she makes. Two, the average, or effective, tax rate comes from dividing the taxpayer's total tax by her total income (or consumption or wages or whatever the tax base is.)

Table 5.1 Bedrock's Tax Rate Schedule

INCOME ($)	TAX RATE (%)
0–20,000	0
20,000–60,000	15
over 60,000	30

Suppose a taxpayer pays $4,000 tax on $40,000 of income. Her average tax is 10 percent, $4,000 divided by $40,000.

A simple example will help you to see this better.

Meet the Flintstones

Meet the Flintstones, a typical family of four. (For true Flintstones fans, imagine that somewhere along the line Pebbles gained a little brother.) Suppose that Fred, the father and breadwinner, earns $20,000 a year from his job at the local quarry. There is a fairly simple income tax in place for families of four in Bedrock, as shown in table 5.1. At $20,000 of total income, the Flintstones pay no income tax. All of their income falls in the zero bracket. But suppose that Fred gets a raise to $30,000 a year. How much tax will the Flintstones pay? The correct answer is $1,500. When his income passed $20,000 Fred entered the 15 percent rate bracket. This means that his marginal tax rate—the rate that his next dollar of income bears—is 15 percent. It does *not* mean that all of Fred's $30,000 will get taxed at the 15 percent rate. The Flintstones will never pay tax on the part of their income that falls within the zero bracket— $20,000 in this example—even if Fred's earnings take them above it.

This points to a common misunderstanding of how taxes work— the tendency to confuse marginal and average tax rates. People sometimes think that they shouldn't earn any more money because doing so will push them into a higher tax bracket and they will end up losing money in the end. But entering a new rate bracket doesn't mean that you are taxed more heavily on what you were already making. Rate brackets work like a ladder. As you climb the income ladder, you still get to keep the benefits of the lower rungs. So when Fred makes $30,000, the Flintstones still pay no tax on their *first* $20,000 of income—the income that takes them from $0 to $20,000. They pay 15 percent only on their *next* $10,000—the income that takes them from $20,000 to $30,000. As long as marginal tax rates stay below 100 percent, taxes won't ever cause you to lose money by making more.

When a rate structure uses marginal brackets, a taxpayer's average tax rate is almost always different from his marginal rate. When the Flintstones make $30,000 as a family and pay $1,500 in taxes, their average tax rate is 5 percent—$1,500 divided by $30,000 in income. The Flintstones get to keep ninety-five cents out of every dollar that Fred earns on average. But this doesn't change the fact that the Flintstones are now in the 15 percent bracket. If Fred got an additional raise, of $1,000, the family would pay $150 of that increment in taxes.

Marginal and average rates are two different concepts. Both kinds of rates are important in thinking about tax.

Why Marginal Tax Rates Matter

Marginal rates are important for individual decision making. Suppose Fred keeps working harder and is earning $60,000 a year with overtime. His boss offers Fred the chance to work on a particular Sunday for an extra $1,000. But this would mean Fred would have to cancel plans to go bowling with his pal Barney Rubble. When figuring out what to do, Fred calculates that he will only really receive $700 for his day of work. That's because once he has made $60,000, Fred enters the 30 percent bracket. He will have to pay 30 percent, or $300, in taxes on the $1,000 that takes him from $60,000 to $61,000 in total income. This marginal disincentive may cause Fred to decide not to work and to go bowling with Barney instead.

A big part of the trouble with an income tax is that its marginal disincentives fall on individual work and saving. These high marginal rates trap the working classes: they make it hard to escape the rat race, to save enough to move beyond a paycheck-to-paycheck existence.

Marginal rates also are important to possible second earners, like Wilma, as they consider whether to work outside the home. This was a major theme in my first book, *Taxing Women*, where I explored the ways in which U.S. tax laws make it difficult to be a married working mother, notwithstanding the fact that most American mothers now do work for pay outside (as well as for no pay inside) the home.

The common theme here is that in a very practical sense, we all live and make our important life decisions on the margin. Marginal rates matter.

Why Average Tax Rates Matter

Average tax rates matter for different reasons. Logically, they should not affect individual decisions. When Fred was making $30,000 and paying an average tax of 5 percent, he would have been wrong if he thought that he could take home 95 percent of the *next* dollar he earned. Average tax rates do not matter for individual decision making, but they do point to the overall distribution and fairness of tax burdens.

Because America taxes about one-third of its GDP with all federal, state, and local taxes combined, the average tax rate for Americans as a whole is 33 percent. (The average tax rate under the federal income tax alone is, of course, far less—currently under 9 percent.) But this doesn't mean that each and every American pays this much. Some pay more, others less. Looking at patterns of average tax rates helps us to determine how the overall tax burden varies with income or wealth. If the richest Americans were paying a 40 percent average rate across all taxes, then the middle and lower classes would be able to pay less and still get the country to the overall 33 percent figure. Average tax rates matter for analyzing the fairness of tax.

Progressivity and Regressivity

A tax system can be progressive, flat, or regressive. A progressive tax is one in which the rich pay a higher average rate than the not-rich. A flat, or proportionate, tax is one in which everyone pays the same average rate. A regressive tax is one in which the rich pay a lower average rate than the not-rich.

The current inconsistent income tax features progressive marginal rates. It is thus intended to be a progressive tax. But we now know that things aren't always what they seem to be in tax. The actual pattern of a tax system's progressivity depends on what sort of loopholes and gaps the tax has and on who can take advantage of them.

Table 5.2 Income, Payroll, and Combined Marginal Tax Rates
(approx.) for an Individual, circa 2001

INCOME ($)	MARGINAL INCOME TAX RATE (%)	PAYROLL TAX RATE (%)	COMBINED MARGINAL TAX RATE (%)
0–10,000	0	15	15
10,000–30,000	15	15	30
30,000–60,000	28	15	43
60,000–80,000	31	15	46
80,000–125,000	31	3	34
125,000–250,000	36	3	39
over 250,000	40	3	43

As we have seen—and as Rich Dad knows perfectly well—the progressive marginal rates of the inconsistent income tax fall on earnings from work and the realized yield to savings. If we look at reported wages and investment gains, therefore, we would expect to find a progressive average pattern. We do. But if we look instead to all the money a particular taxpayer has to spend, it is no longer clear that the inconsistent income tax is progressive at all. Artful Dodger and Lear's eldest daughters paid no taxes under the present income tax, notwithstanding their lavish lifestyles; Rich Dad and many millionaires next door are not far off. It hardly seems progressive to have rich spenders bear an average tax rate of zero percent.

The system is even less progressive when we factor in the payroll tax, as tables 5.2 and 5.3 show. It's difficult to construct such tables, because people's tax situations vary so much, but these should give you the general idea, again using round numbers. As explained in chapter 1, I'm using the full 15 percent payroll tax, adding together both the employer's and the employee's shares. This tax applies in full until a taxpayer has earned about $80,000 in wages, when it drops to the Medicare portion alone, around 3 percent.

These tables show that even looking at reported income alone, the American tax system isn't all that progressive today. A recent academic analysis concluded that the overall distribution of American taxes changed very little from 1979 to 2000, although the income tax became, ostensibly at least, more progressive during that time.

Table 5.3 Income, Payroll, and Combined Marginal Tax Rates
(approx.) for a Family of Four with Two Equal Earners, circa 2001

INCOME ($)	MARGINAL INCOME TAX RATE (%)	PAYROLL TAX RATE (%)	COMBINED MARGINAL TAX RATE (%)
0–20,000	0	15	15
20,000–60,000	15	15	30
60,000–110,000	28	15	43
110,000–160,000	31	15	46
160,000–250,000	36	3	39
over 250,000	40	3	43

This is because the burden of the payroll tax system grew over the same twenty-year period—and the payroll tax is a regressive one. Yet tax cuts virtually always mean income tax cuts in American political lingo. The payroll tax has not once been reduced since its birth in the 1930s.

Back to Bedrock

Note that we can have a pattern of progressive average rates by combining a flat marginal rate with a rebate. Imagine that President Slate imposed a flat 20 percent income tax on the citizens of Bedrock. He also sets up a program to give every person a rebate of her taxes, up to $1,000. Consider the net effect of such a system on a family of four like the Flintstones, who can get a rebate of up to $4,000, $1,000 for each individual family member.

Table 5.4 shows the Flintstones' tax, rebate, net tax, and average tax rate at different levels of income. Note how easily I constructed this chart. The tax is simply 20 percent of income. The rebate is $4,000 or the amount of the tax, whichever is lower. (The rebate can reduce the tax to zero, but not below.) By subtracting the rebate from the tax owed, we get the net tax amount. Finally, by dividing the net tax by the family's total income, we get to the average tax rate.

The table shows that we can have a pattern of progressive average tax rates without depending on progressive marginal ones. Until the Flintstones have made $20,000, they pay no net tax—the rebate wipes out the 20 percent tax. Thereafter, although Fred continues to

Table 5.4 Bedrock's Flat Tax plus Rebate

FAMILY INCOME ($)	TAX AT 20% ($)	REBATE ($)	NET TAX ($)	AVERAGE TAX RATE (%)
0	0	0	0	0
10,000	2,000	2,000	0	0
20,000	4,000	4,000	0	0
30,000	6,000	4,000	2,000	6.7
50,000	10,000	4,000	6,000	12.0
100,000	20,000	4,000	16,000	16.0
200,000	40,000	4,000	36,000	18.0

face a flat marginal rate of 20 percent, his average rate is much lower because the rebate has knocked off the tax on the first $20,000. The average rate steadily rises with income—it approaches, but never quite gets to, 20 percent. Thus this is a progressive tax system, but it does not have progressive marginal rates.

Figure 5.1 puts these same results in picture form. It shows the average tax rate of a family of four in Bedrock as their income rises: the rate is zero percent until they earn $20,000, and thereafter it steadily rises, even though the marginal rate stays flat at 20 percent. This picture also illustrates how the common flat-tax plans from chapter 3 work. An exempt range plus a single positive rate bracket generates a pattern of progressive average rates.

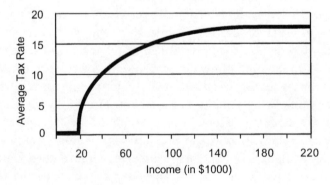

Progressivity in Bedrock

Figure 5.1 Effect of Flat Tax plus Rebate

THE PARADOX OF PROGRESSIVITY

Assume for the time being that fairness requires a progressive pattern of average rates: the wealthy should pay a somewhat higher average tax rate than the nonwealthy. A majority of Americans seem to agree. The desire for progressivity, however, poses a dilemma for tax reformers. It is a basic principle of economic theory and common sense that high marginal rates highly distort individual decision making.

Recall from our brief tour of tax history in chapter 1 that the top marginal income tax bracket in America has been as high as 94 percent. The top bracket stayed at or above 90 percent throughout the 1950s and lingered at 70 percent following John F. Kennedy's 1963 tax cut all the way to Ronald Reagan's presidency. It doesn't take a rocket scientist to see that there is something wrong with rates that high: many Americans would rather stay home at the margin (or go bowling) than see ninety or seventy cents out of every additional dollar they earn go to the government.

If we aim for fairness by having high marginal rates under an income tax, we have to live with these distorting effects. Those citizens capable of earning the highest wages or reaping the greatest returns to capital would be the most discouraged from additional productive activity. Many ordinary Americans would be dissuaded from working overtime or taking on a second job to help their families get ahead. In many two-parent households a second wage earner, most often the wife, would face heavy tax rates on paid work outside the home. It seems as though we are in the grip of a fatal trade-off between fairness and efficiency. Fairness suggests higher tax rates; efficiency counsels against them.

Indeed, this practical dilemma has led to a tax system today in which the top rate brackets are not all that progressive, in historical terms. Look again at tables 5.2 and 5.3. Under the income tax alone, the lowest rate bracket—the 15 percent one—kicks in early. The highest marginal tax rate is now just under 40 percent (and declining under the George W. Bush tax plan), far below its historical high of 94 percent. Further, all taxpayers making $250,000 or more are in this highest marginal rate bracket; there are no additional brackets at, say, $500,000 or $1 million or more. The relative compression of the rate brackets means that the middle and upper-middle classes get squeezed hard.

The squeeze is even tighter when payroll taxes are added in. Look at table 5.2. A single person making between $30,000 and $80,000 pays well over 40 percent of her marginal earnings to the federal government; add in any kind of state or local tax and she's at a 50 percent marginal rate. These tables do not even reflect an increasingly important effect confronting the working poor. As the lower-income classes earn wages, their various government benefits are phased out. This is identical in effect to a marginal tax: as you earn money, the government takes away money you would otherwise have. This phenomenon, little known by the middle and upper classes, can be severe. The working poor—especially working single parents—can face effective marginal tax rates exceeding 100 percent.

This is all bleak news for the cause of progressivity in tax. The good news is that we don't have to live with the trade-offs that our inconsistent income tax poses for us.

It is time to reconnect the tax base and rate discussions. The tax base is the *what* that is being distorted by the high marginal tax rates. High marginal tax rates under a consistent income tax discourage high-end individual work and savings. In contrast, high consumption tax rates under a postpaid consumption, or spending, tax discourage high-end individual spending. The nature of the tax base affects the nature of the argument for progressive tax rates. Whereas no sensible person should want the distortions of individual choices generated by an income tax, a consumption tax is another matter— it is not necessarily a bad thing to dissuade rich people from spending lots of money on themselves.

In hindsight, advocates of economic progressivity made a mistake when they chose an income tax to finance the burdens of a modern democratic state. They compounded their error by choosing steeply progressive marginal rates. They had to back off almost immediately from a consistent income tax, for what wealthy person would save and incur double taxes at the 70 or 90 percent level? So tax rates on capital were slashed, when we taxed capital at all. In time, the income tax became a wage tax, with lingering high rates. But this progressive wage tax could never get too progressive or the rich would stop working and stay home. So we ended up with a tax that quickly reached a high rate on the middle classes—folks with no choice but to work.

The Fair Not Flat Tax gets out of this dilemma by moving the tax system consistently and consciously to a progressive spending tax. This changes things. When taxes no longer fall on work and savings but on spending, the argument for progressive rates is different— and, I believe, much stronger.

THE FAIRNESS OF A PROGRESSIVE SPENDING TAX

So far I have only posited the fairness of a progressive spending tax. Now it's time to argue it out. This is challenging, because experience and common sense have taught me abundantly well that not all minds can be changed on this score: some folks are just die-hard flat-taxers. But I will try to persuade even these adamant opponents of progressivity.

Let's begin with their own plans. Remember the zero bracket of the flat-tax proposals we looked at in chapter 3? The logic of such a zero bracket under an income or wage tax—recall that the flat-tax plans were in fact wage taxes—is that the first $20,000 or so of a typical family's earnings are entitled to a lower tax rate. Presumably this is because these earnings are most likely to be spent on life's necessities, such as food, clothing, and shelter. Note that even under an income or wage tax structure we are really talking about the uses of wealth.

It's a bit difficult to continue to argue in this vein to justify higher tax rates on higher levels of income. We would need to say that higher levels of earnings are less essential to the earner—or, in keeping with traditional income tax language, somehow reflect a greater "ability to pay"—than lower levels of earnings. But what about ordinary workers who put in overtime or work two jobs to save up for some future need, such as their children's college education? Two-earner families particularly struggle under the weight of an onerous wage tax system that has little in the way of deductions or other

provisions to help offset the high after-tax costs of child care. Arguing for a progressive tax on inflows is challenging.

Note how the logic and rhetoric change when personal spending
becomes the tax base. The argument for the zero bracket is now considerably more straightforward: the first $20,000 of spending by a
family of four is likely to go toward life's necessities and thus should
bear no burden of tax. Here we have our first principle of the fair
rate structure under a consistent spending tax:

Spending on life's necessities should bear little or no tax.

Because there's little difference between earnings and spending at
the lowest income levels, the argument looks like the one accepted
by income- and flat-tax supporters alike.

But spending over a certain minimum is more discretionary and
reflects a greater ability to pay taxes, to help pay for public goods.
And so a second principle of the fair rate structure is:

**Spending on ordinary consumer items should bear a higher rate
of tax than spending on life's necessities.**

Notice how it is far more persuasive to continue the argument for
progressivity under a postpaid consumption tax than under an income or wage tax. Whereas we were dubious about the relative importance of *earnings* at different levels, we can plausibly say that
spending above certain levels becomes less urgent or important or
at least more able to bear a tax.

Now we can continue. High-end spenders can—and indeed
should—pay a higher rate of tax at the margins of their lifestyle. It
is easy enough to suggest, for example, that a family of four that
spends more than $80,000 a year on itself should pay a higher rate
of taxes at the margin—that is, a higher rate of taxes on its least
important purchases—than a family spending half as much. Just as
the first dollars of spending should bear a lower rate or no tax at all
because they purchase the most basic and essential goods and services, so too the last dollars spent by a wealthy household should
bear a higher rate of tax because they are purchasing luxury items.
Here is the third and final principle of the fair rate structure:

Spending on luxuries should bear a higher rate of tax than spending on ordinary consumer items.

That's how one argues for a fair rate structure under a consistent spending tax such as the Fair Not Flat Tax.

I haven't yet defined *life's necessities, ordinary consumer items,* or *luxuries*. Some readers no doubt will consider this a hopeless task. But a large part of the beauty of the Fair Not Flat Tax is that we do not have to be terribly specific in defining the different types of spending—almost all of the work gets done in setting rate brackets.

Matters of Kind and Degree

There is nothing alien in making judgments about the relative importance of different expenditures. When today's income tax allows a deduction for extraordinary medical expenses or charitable contributions, it is making judgments about kinds of consumption. When it sets rate levels, it is making judgments about degrees of consumption.

A consistent spending tax can more sensibly make distinctions of both degree and kind. As a matter of kind, we can carve out certain uses of our money—home mortgage interest, charitable contributions, and payments for medical expenses and education—as being inappropriate to tax. As a matter of degree, we can say that different levels of spending roughly reflect different levels of importance or urgency. Just as we can use this logic to argue for a zero bracket at the bottom, so too we can use it to argue for higher rates at the top.

Some economically minded readers may object that all high earners are in fact high spenders: that the only reason to earn a large amount of money in the first place is to be able to spend it all on oneself. If so, the disincentives under a progressive spending tax become the same as those under an income tax. The facts of the matter contradict the case: not all high earners are high spenders. A large majority of wealthy Americans do not spend all of their available resources on themselves. While the lower and middle classes in America do not save much money, the upper classes do—and saving means not consuming. This is one of the most important lessons of *The Millionaire Next Door.*

The Fair Not Flat Tax allows and encourages the most common form of lifestyle among America's rich: a prudent, frugal one with some intergenerational altruism. Whereas the incentives of the current estate and income taxes are to spend it all now and die broke, the incentives under the Fair Not Flat Tax are to keep saving, within and across generations. This is not to say that the Fair Not Flat Tax will never discourage or distort individual behavior. Any tax will. A progressive spending tax has its disincentive effects. But these disincentives fall only on the high spenders among the rich, not on every single wealthy person—and not directly on the beneficial activities of work and savings. By virtue of their thrift King Lear, his favored Cordelia, and a good many millionaires next door will escape the burden of higher tax rates, whereas the prodigal Regan, her sister Goneril, and scores of die-brokers will not. The best argument for the Fair Not Flat Tax is not that it is the least onerous tax across the board. It is that it has the right, or most fair, set of incentives and disincentives.

Giving the Rich a Choice

A progressive spending tax expects the rich to help out their community, but it gives them a choice of how to do so. The fortunate can save some of their wealth and thereby help everyone by contributing to the capital stock. Savings help to keep interest rates low, benefiting students and homeowners, among others. Savings also help to provide for our nation's future—for our children and our children's children. A consistent, progressive spending tax ought to make it easier for the lower and middle classes to consume by putting more of the responsibility for the nation's savings on the shoulders of the rich. And the whole society should *want* the rich to save. This moves us toward a model of class teamwork and away from class conflict.

The fortunate few are not, however, forced to save under the Fair Not Flat Tax. It's a free country, and the rich will have a choice. They can go ahead and spend all or most of their money on personal consumption items; they will simply incur an added tax for the privilege as they do so. The rich make the choice of how to contribute

Table 5.5 Fair Not Flat Tax Rate Schedule
for a Family of Four

Spending ($)	Tax Rate (%)
0–20,000	0
20,000–80,000	10
80,000–160,000	20
160,000–500,000	30
500,000–1,000,000	40
over 1,000,000	50

to society—by saving or by spending and paying the progressive spending tax. Under the Fair Not Flat Tax, it will simply no longer be possible to live the luxurious life without paying the tax collector's toll.

PUTTING SOME NUMBERS ON THE TABLE

I never planned to write the kind of numbers-filled tome that blue ribbon commissions produce and no one reads. My aim has been to help general readers understand the big picture of tax policy today: why we do not and should not have an income tax, and why we could and should have a consistent, progressive spending tax. But just to provide a rough sense of the kind of thing I am talking about, I will propose an approximate rate structure for the Fair Not Flat Tax.

In coming up with these numbers, I have tried to make a guess at revenue-neutral rates; that is, I have tried to estimate rates that will generate the same revenue as the current income tax does. This is a bit difficult because there are proposals pending to cut income tax rates as I write, but such is life as a tax expert. My other self-imposed limitation is never to have a marginal tax rate over 50 percent. Even for the richest American's last dollar of spending, one-half sounds high enough. With these guidelines in mind, I have come up with a rough estimate of a fair rate structure for a family of four. It is shown in table 5.5. Most Americans would pay the Fair Not Flat Tax at the basic 10 percent rate, though their average tax rate, as we have seen, would be less. (But note that I have retained the payroll tax.) Only the wealthiest minority would pay more than that, and they would pay it on discretionary spending, not on work or savings.

Smoke and Mirrors?

Academics and policymakers commonly assert that tax rates would have to rise under a transition to a consumption tax. Because an income tax includes savings in its base and a consumption tax does not, they argue, tax rates must go up under a consumption tax to keep government revenues constant. But the Fair Not Flat Tax rate structure I have just sketched out has a 10 percent bracket that is far wider than the 15 percent bracket under the current income tax. How can this be?

Once again, I am not a formal economic modeler, and I don't want this book to get bogged down in a quagmire of numeric arguments. I readily admit that my numbers may be optimistic. Perhaps the 10 percent rate ought to be 12 or even 15 percent; perhaps its range ought to be smaller. But I do want to defend my estimate and note that the common wisdom that a consumption tax must have higher rates is misleading, for four main reasons.

One, we don't have a consistent income tax. We're not even close to having one. Because today's inconsistent income tax already fails to tax most savings, a consistent consumption tax won't let too much more wealth escape from its base by having a consistent, unlimited deduction for savings.

Two, a consistent spending tax such as the Fair Not Flat Tax has a very important base-broadening feature compared to the status quo: the inclusion of debt-financed consumption. The Fair Not Flat Tax shuts down Tax Planning 101. Because it includes debt in its base, it eliminates step two in the "buy, borrow, die" tax plan. And so the super-rich can no longer spend high and live well tax free. Middle-class consumer debt will also be taxed at the moment it's incurred. Once again, I have no precise way of determining the amount that debt-financed consumption would add to the tax base, but there is reason to believe it is considerable.

Three, there is no need for a capital gains preference under the Fair Not Flat Tax. Indeed, there is no need for the concept of basis or for the realization requirement or any of the other complex rules

Table 5.6 Fair Not Flat, Payroll, and Combined Tax Rates
for a Family of Four

INCOME ($)	MARGINAL FAIR NOT FLAT TAX RATE (%)	PAYROLL TAX RATE (%)	COMBINED MARGINAL TAX RATE (%)
0–20,000	0	15	15
20,000–80,000	10	15	25
80,000–160,000	20	15	35
160,000–500,000	30	3	33
500,000–1,000,000	40	3	43
over 1,000,000	50	3	53

about capital. Taxpayers can buy, sell, and trade investment assets within their unlimited savings accounts as they deem fit, just as they can do today within their IRAs and 401(k) plans. When they withdraw money to spend, they will pay the spending tax at ordinary rates—again as happens today with IRA plans.

Four, although the increase is hardly radical, my preferred Fair Not Flat Tax does add to existing law's 40 percent rate for the highest spenders. Families that spend $1 million or more in a year will face a marginal tax rate of 50 percent.

In time it might be possible to move away from the payroll tax and to build up the progressive spending tax. In my rough calculations, I have left the payroll tax in place for now. I constructed table 5.6 on the basis of the simplifying assumption that all wages are consumed. If you compare it with table 5.3, you will see that the burden on the lower and middle classes eases. It may appear at first that there is also some diminished progressivity for the upper-middle class. But recall that Tax Planning 101 will cease and the capital gains preference will disappear. Real spending will bear real taxes.

As I've said, this rate structure represents a crude guess, and I await a rash of technical analysis improving it. But the principles are what count at this stage. And the Fair Not Flat Tax is far more principled than the mess of a tax we have today.

THE OTHER SIDE OF THE COIN

All of these arguments for progressively taxing consumption have a logical flip side. A consistent postpaid consumption tax falls on spending, not on savings. We have seen that savings are good on both a personal and a social level for various reasons. The Haig-Simons definition, Income = Consumption + Savings, helps us to see an interesting fact:

> **Savings are nonconsumption. If we want**
> **savings, we must have nonconsumption.**

The question of providing for the nation's total supply of savings thus becomes one of asking who should consume less in order to fund society's reasonable capital stock requirements. The flip side to the question of what consumption should we tax is what nonconsumption should we encourage? The Fair Not Flat Tax's answer is compelling: it is the wealthy who should consume less. This would free up the lower and middle classes to consume more.

THE USUAL OBJECTIONS

Perhaps you've noticed by now that I have few fully committed allies in my quest for a better, fairer tax system. My liberal friends, whom I've addressed in prior chapters, typically object to the idea of consumption taxes. My conservative friends typically object to the idea of progressive rates. "Progressive rates? Why, that's like socialism! You're just soaking the rich. It's all a matter of envy," many of them have repeatedly told me.

I have found that conservative objections to progressive rates are not as easily answered as liberal concerns about consumption taxes— we could see that liberal goals could best be served by means other than our current system. Still, there are a couple of responses that might help to assuage conservative critics.

One, I am only discussing replacing the income tax. Important as it is, it accounts for only about one-fifth of all taxes in America today. Payroll, business, and state and local sales taxes are also very important taxes, and these have little or no elements of progressivity in them. We've already seen that the Social Security contribution works like a flat-rate tax on wages, with no zero bracket or accommodations for family size, medical expenses, or the like. Worse, because the payroll tax is cut off at a certain level of income, now about $80,000, it is actually regressive at the highest levels of earnings. The puzzle of business taxes is that no one is quite sure who really pays them. A business is not a flesh-and-blood human being, so any tax that it pays must ultimately come from someone—most likely out of the pockets of ordinary workers and consumers. State and local sales taxes are all flat-rate ones. Our principal federal tax system is the only place to get any progressivity at all in tax. The relatively modest degree of progressivity in the Fair Not Flat Tax system is likely to bring about a relatively even net distribution of taxes between the middle and upper classes.

Two, the Fair Not Flat Tax abolishes the inconsistent income tax as well as the dreaded death tax. These reforms benefit the wealthy. Capital gains, interest and dividends, and estates will no longer be taxed. The rich will no longer need to face the transaction costs of setting up their affairs to minimize these taxes. Artful Dodger's tax advisers will be put out of business. Costly and complicated estate tax avoidance plans will no longer be necessary. Wealthy savers will be able to move their assets freely among different investments with no tax toll on the sale or exchange. These are all enormous benefits to the wealthy when measured against the disaster of the status quo. The progressive rates of the Fair Not Flat Tax can be thought of as the price the wealthy must pay for these very important changes; it is the great trade-off in the new tax. In political terms, the Fair Not Flat Tax agrees with conservatives about the tax base and with liberals, or at least with moderates, about tax rates.

Not all wealthy people will or should object to my proposal. I know from firsthand experience that many wealthy citizens will prefer the Fair Not Flat Tax to the status quo—and not just because it is more principled and sensible than our current mess of a tax. Many wealthy people will actually see their taxes decrease under the Fair Not Flat Tax; only some will see them rise. Who will win and who will lose? The winners will be none other than the savers—the Ants, Cordelia Lears, and millionaires next door. The spenders—the Grasshoppers, Artful Dodgers, and die-brokers—will lose out.

People who are building up estates or family businesses in order to pass them on to their children will be able to die in peace, without fear that the tax collector will dance on their graves.

Taxes need to be paid. Today the working classes are disproportionately paying them. To reverse this means raising tax rates a bit on high spenders, many of whom are perfectly legally paying little or no taxes today. Taxes are, after all, the price of civilization. The wealthy have civilization aplenty. It's only fair to ask them to pay their fair share for it.

The Fair Not Flat Tax

In tax reform, then, history teaches us that boldness pays. Taxpayers may well suffer less under radical reform than under a blizzard of piecemeal changes.

—Carl S. Shoup, introduction to *Blueprints for Basic Tax Reform*

THE PATH TO SENSIBLE TAX REFORM IS NOW CLEAR. WE should replace the inconsistent income and ineffective estate taxes with a single, consistent, progressive spending tax: the Fair Not Flat Tax.

This isn't nearly as hard to do as it sounds. The current income tax is already largely a consumption tax. We will start with it, bearing in mind that Consumption = Income − Savings. Four simple steps can take us to the promised land of a better, simpler tax:

1. Include borrowing as income
2. Allow unlimited deductions for contributions to savings accounts; tax withdrawals from such accounts
3. Repeal the special capital gains rate
4. Repeal the gift and estate tax

That's it. Take these four steps, and we have a consistent, progressive spending tax. We can get rid of lots of other rules along the way— all of the stuff about basis, realization, and so on that the inconsistent income tax has spawned. In the meantime, we can keep or even increase progressivity in tax rates. We'll have a better, simpler, fairer system overnight.

97

CALCULATING THE FAIR NOT FLAT TAX

The Fair Not Flat Tax is moderate in many ways. Life won't change all that much for most Americans. The major practical difference under the new law will be that taxpayers who save won't have to worry any more about complicated rules like limits on IRAs or the details of how their savings and investment transactions are taxed. For the majority of Americans, who don't save, there will be even less change. They will pay tax on their earnings as usual.

Before long, I will propose a way to simplify life even more for most Americans by substituting a national sales tax or VAT for the lowest positive rate bracket of the Fair Not Flat Tax. But for now, let's assume that the system will continue to operate on an annual return basis. Taxpayers will fill out a Fair Tax form that will be only slightly different from the present 1040. On a Fair Tax form you will start with the W-2s that you already receive each January telling you what your wages were for the year before. You will also have D-2 forms to reflect your net borrowing for the year; you would get these from credit card companies and banks. Finally, you will have S-2 forms for your savings accounts. To mark a distinction with the current law's IRAs, which have complex rules for payments in and distributions out, I will call these tax-favored savings accounts *Trust Accounts*. Contributions to Trust Accounts will appear as positive numbers on S-2s; withdrawals will appear as negative numbers. You won't need all of the 1099 forms that show dividends and interest and so forth, because the relevant savings and investment activity takes place inside the Trust Accounts. The Fair Not Flat Tax considers only what you put in and what you take out of such accounts.

To fill out your Fair Tax form, you will simply gather together these forms and calculate as follows:

W-2s (Wages) + D-2s (Debts) − S-2s (Savings) = Taxable Consumption

We can refine this basic picture as much as we wanted. We can allow whatever subtractions from taxable consumption that we think fair and fitting: deductions or credits for medical expenses, charitable contributions, and home mortgage interest, for example, all just as we do now under the inconsistent income tax. As an important bonus under the new law, debate about whether a certain type of expense should be deductible will be one in which most Americans can participate. It's all really pretty simple, in principle and in practice. I discuss more technical matters in the Questions and Comments, but these don't obscure the basic simplicity of the plan. We will no longer need to allow preferences for particular types of savings, because the Fair Not Flat Tax systematically exempts all savings. There will be no need for special rules for pension plans, capital gains, tax-free municipal bonds, and so forth. The law will be vastly simpler and more understandable than it is now.

Once you have performed the basic calculations and taken whatever additional deductions lawmakers have seen fit to grant, you end up with your taxable consumption or spending for the prior year. Then you will calculate your tax according a progressive rate structure like the one I outlined in table 5-5.

THE FAIR NOT FLAT TAX IN ACTION

Suppose that in one particular year George and Louise Jefferson earned $35,000, borrowed $10,000, and put $5,000 into their Trust Account. Their taxable consumption, or spending, for the year would be:

$$\$35,000 + 10,000 - 5,000 = \$40,000$$

The Jeffersons' tax would be calculated on $40,000, reflecting what they spent during the year. Their first $20,000 of consumption would generate no tax because it falls in the zero bracket. They would pay a 10 percent tax on the next $20,000, producing a total tax of $2,000.

If, on the other hand, the Jeffersons had borrowed only $5,000 and saved $10,000, they would discover how the Fair Not Flat Tax benefits savers. Their taxable consumption for the year would be:

$$\$35,000 + \$5,000 - \$10,000 = \$30,000$$

Because of the rebate, they would be paying the 10 percent sales tax on only $10,000 of their spending, so their total tax would be $1,000—representing a $1,000 decrease in their tax bill.

SIMPLIFY, SIMPLIFY, SIMPLIFY

OK, it's time to make things even simpler, without changing the basic nature of the Fair Not Flat Tax. The tax is a consistent, postpaid consumption tax. In chapter 3 we learned that sales taxes and VATs are also such taxes and that rebates or credits can be used to achieve the same effect as a zero bracket. These facts give us an easy way to knock the two lowest rate brackets off of the Fair Not Flat Tax so that most Americans will no longer have to fill out annual forms.

We can impose a national sales tax or VAT at a uniform 10 percent rate. There are, of course, numerous practical and administrative issues involved in deciding which one to use. I touched on these briefly in chapter 3. For now let's keep putting the grittiest details aside. The important point is that we can use the functional equivalence of sales taxes, VATs, and other forms of postpaid consumption taxes to simplify the Fair Not Flat Tax for most taxpayers.

A TECHNICAL POINT

Technically, if we were to substitute a national sales tax or VAT for the lowest positive rate bracket of the Fair Not Flat Tax, its rate would have to be higher than 10 percent to keep revenues constant. This is because broad-based taxes such as the current income one are tax-inclusive. This means that the tax paid is part of the base. When you pay a 10 percent tax on $10,000 of earnings, you don't actually get to take home $10,000. The tax comes out of this gross amount, and you only take home $9,000.

In contrast, sales taxes are tax-exclusive taxes. The tax is not part of the base. When you pay a 10 percent sales tax on a one-dollar candy bar, for example, you must reach into your pocket and pull out an additional ten cents.

It is easy enough to convert from a tax-inclusive rate to a tax-exclusive one. One dollar subject to a 10 percent tax-inclusive rate would net a taxpayer ninety cents. So she is really paying 11 percent of what she keeps, ten divided by ninety. This is the equivalent rate that a national sales tax would have to have to replace a 10 percent bracket. For the sake of simplicity, though, I will refer to a 10 percent sales tax or VAT in the text.

Table 6.1 Rate Schedule for the Supplemental
Personal Consumption Tax for a Family of Four

SPENDING ($)	TAX RATE (%)
0–80,000	0
80,000–160,000	10
160,000–500,000	20
500,000–1,000,000	30
over 1,000,000	40

To replicate the effect of a zero bracket, we can allow a credit against the sales tax or VAT. The credit will be set at 10 percent of earnings up to $20,000 for a family of four. In other words, we give the family $2,000 back on a showing that they earned at least $20,000. We can do this by mailing a check; making an automatic deposit into a bank account; giving a credit along with each employee's paycheck; or creating an exemption under the Social Security system, which now operates as a large flat tax on American workers without a zero bracket. However we deliver it, this rebate will offset the 10 percent sales tax on consumption below $20,000, thereby effectively creating a zero bracket. The national sales tax or VAT will then work as a flat 10 percent tax on all consumption above that exempt level.

Finally, because everyone will be paying the sales tax or VAT on spending, we can simply subtract 10 percent from each rate in the Fair Not Flat Tax rate schedule in table 5.5. We are left with a supplemental consumption tax for wealthier families, at the rates shown in table 6.1. Its $80,000 zero bracket, or exemption level, for a family of four means that the vast majority of Americans will not have to complete much paperwork each year. The only people who will directly experience most of the complexity of the tax system will be relatively wealthy people, who presumably can afford advice in meeting their tax obligations. Nor would this supplemental personal spending tax even be all that complex: as we've seen, it's far simpler than the inconsistent income tax. And the personal consumption tax rates would be moderate: 10, 20, 30, and 40 percent, the highest rate being only for expenditures over $1 million a year.

IN OTHER WORDS: A PROGRESSIVE
NATIONAL SALES TAX

The Fair Not Flat Tax is in essence a progressive national sales tax. Families are taxed on their spending decisions. Families of four are not taxed at all on their first $20,000 of spending because of the rebate. On their next $60,000—up to spending of $80,000 a year— they are taxed at a flat 10 percent rate under the national sales tax or VAT. Above that, families will pay a supplemental personal consumption tax at marginal rates of 10, 20, 30, or 40 percent. Add it all together, and we have a progressive tax on spending.

CONSISTENCY

It's pretty easy to situate the Fair Not Flat Tax in today's tax reform climate. The new tax may sound strange to anyone unfamiliar with the many nuances of tax policy. But it is not. Consider two broad camps of contemporary tax reformers.

Most liberals and Democrats ostensibly support the status quo, with its income-plus-estate tax. In fact, however, most members of this camp also advocate enough pro-savings provisions for the middle and lower classes that they end up advocating a consumption tax for the not-rich. Because the income of the vast majority of Americans falls only in the zero or 15 percent brackets, this looks a lot like the so-called flat-tax plans we looked at in chapter 3, with their two tax rates and consumption bases. Michael Graetz, a fairly liberal Yale law professor, suggests in his recent book, *The Decline (and Fall?) of the U.S. Income Tax*, that we institute a VAT plus a rebate for the middle classes while retaining the income-plus-estate tax for the rich. Liberals are consistent in their choice of a progressive rate structure but inconsistent in their choice of tax base.

Conservatives and Republicans, in contrast, are consistent advocates of a consumption base, but inconsistent when it comes to rates. The flat-tax plans are two-rate consumption taxes that are effectively progressive among the lower and middle classes but then flatten out for the rich. Recall figure 5.1 from the Bedrock example, which shows how a two-rate plan is progressive over lower- and middle-class, but not upper-class, ranges of income.

Table 6.2 Liberal, Conservative, and Fair Not Flat Tax Policies

		BASE	RATES
LIBERAL TAX POLICY	NOT-RICH	Consumption	Progressive
	RICH	Income plus estate	Progressive
CONSERVATIVE TAX POLICY	NOT-RICH	Consumption	Progressive
	RICH	Consumption	Flat
FAIR NOT FLAT TAX POLICY	NOT-RICH	Consumption	Progressive
	RICH	Consumption	Progressive

What's striking is that both camps agree on how to tax most Americans, the overwhelming majority of whom never see their income rise above today's 15 percent bracket. Liberals and conservatives, Democrats and Republicans all pretty much agree that we should have a two-rate consumption tax for the not-rich. Where the political factions fight it out is only about how to tax the rich, with liberals wanting a progressive income-plus-estate tax and conservatives a flat consumption tax.

The Fair Not Flat Tax splits the difference while sticking to its principles. It's a consistent, progressive spending tax on all classes of Americans. Table 6.2 makes the point by comparing liberal, conservative, and Fair Not Flat Tax policies.

A WORD ON TRUST ACCOUNTS

The Trust Accounts under the Fair Not Flat Tax have many interesting and attractive qualities. For one thing, they make the concept of basis obsolete: basis represents after-tax dollars, and money put into Trust Accounts will not have been taxed. It's just like money you have in a pension plan or IRA. Because that money has never been taxed, it has no basis. It is fully taxable when—but only when—you withdraw it. So too with Trust Accounts.

You will be free to buy and sell assets within your Trust Account without incurring any interim tax. You will also be able to switch from stocks to bonds to real estate and back again as you see fit, just as you now can do inside your IRAs or 401(k)s. All of this is efficient because investment decisions will no longer be affected by tax. There is no lock-in effect.

Another advantage of the Trust Accounts is that they allow society to watch over the investment behavior of the wealthy, however loosely. We do not have to—and would not want to—micromanage private Trust Accounts. But we can certainly impose some general rules on investment actions as we do now for IRAs, pension plans, and the investments of large nonprofit actors, such as universities, museums, and hospitals. We can impose a general diversification requirement or prudent-investor rule to make sure that investments are made wisely, without concentrating power in a single company or industry. We wouldn't allow taxpayers to lobby policymakers or run for elected office using tax-favored Trust Account funds. Such rules will prevent rich savers from using their accounts to unfairly influence political processes.

But perhaps the biggest advantage of the Trust Accounts and their zero basis is that they allow society to monitor the spending decisions of heirs far better than the fatally flawed status quo does. Let's bring back the Lear family to help us see this point.

The Lears Return

Remember Lear's daughters? The eldest, Regan, spent all of her $1 million gift from her daddy nearly immediately, without paying any tax. Goneril was somewhat more prudent. She used financial vehicles to spread her gift out over her life. She thereby avoided a lifetime of work—and also paid no tax. Only Cordelia, the thrifty and prudent youngest daughter, paid any taxes during her lifetime. When Cordelia died, never having touched her father's gift, the government swooped in under the estate tax to take more than half away.

The Fair Not Flat Tax with its Trust Accounts completely reverses these odd results.

Suppose again that all three daughters get $1 million as they turn twenty-one. Under the Fair Not Flat Tax, Lear simply transfers the sum from his Trust Account to one for each daughter.

When Regan, the eldest and most profligate, pulls out all of her money at once to spend lavishly, she will be hit right away by the full force of the progressive rates under the Fair Not Flat Tax. Nearly $400,000 of the money will go to the government.

Goneril, the middle daughter, who spends down her good fortune steadily rather than all at once, also steadily pays her Fair Not Flat

Tax. If she spends $75,000 a year, for example, she will pay over $5,000 a year in taxes under the Fair Not Flat Tax.

Cordelia, however, never does spend any of the $1 million. So she never pays any tax on the gift. Her money grows and grows, untouched by current taxation. Cordelia's large Trust Account is doing a social service, just as her prudent, thrifty lifestyle is—it is contributing to society's capital stock. The account need not be cut in half by taxes, in Cordelia's life or on her death. Her children—King Lear's grandchildren—will inherit large amounts of wealth in their own Trust Accounts. They will then face the same choices that Lear's daughters did: spend now and pay a hefty tax, spend gradually and pay a gradual tax, or don't spend and don't pay any tax.

Please note a very important point: Cordelia has not "escaped" or "avoided" the Fair Not Flat Tax, as the Artful Dodger had escaped the inconsistent income-plus-estate tax. Cordelia doesn't pay any tax only because she doesn't choose to spend Lear's gift money on herself. But the tax doesn't disappear. It lies in wait until the time when someone spends the money. Cordelia isn't getting away with something under the Fair Not Flat Tax. She is simply living a noble, prudent lifestyle and helping everyone else out in the process, while the government preserves its right to tax if and when someone chooses to spend the money.

GETTING THERE, SLOWLY

The Fair Not Flat Tax is a modest change, as are the basic steps that will get us to it. Expanding deductions for contributions to savings accounts only extends a trend that has long been in the works. Repealing the gift and estate tax means abandoning a small, limited, unproductive, and unpopular tax—another change that is in the works as I write. A capital gains tax is simply not needed under a consistent spending tax. The rate structure of the Fair Not Flat Tax represents a moderate return to our past, when tax rates on the wealthiest people were higher than they are now. Indeed, of the incremental steps to implement the Fair Not Flat Tax, only the inclusion of debt is a major departure from the status quo under the income tax. And this step is dictated by the logic of postpaid consumption taxes. It's really just part of treating savings right, for borrowing is dissaving.

This moderation suggests that incremental moves toward tax reform are possible. For example, without grave transitional worries we could:

- increase or altogether remove limits on IRA contributions and
- repeal the gift and estate tax

In exchange for these pro-capital, pro-savings moves, we could also

- raise tax rates at the high end and
- repeal special capital gains rates

But after these changes have been made, Tax Planning 101 will still be possible. In time we will have to begin taxing debt that is used to finance consumption. This is the only truly complex step to be taken, but it is essential to the logic and fairness of the tax.

The Fair Not Flat Tax holds out the appeal of a simple, efficient, and fair tax system that all Americans can understand and endorse, and one that will lighten the record-keeping burdens ordinary people face. Once the Fair Not Flat Tax has emerged incrementally, the move to replace the two lowest rate brackets with a national sales tax or VAT and a rebate is simply an expert's substitution of roughly equivalent forms. Although we will end up in a place where most Americans will no longer have to fill out annual tax returns, and although the current income and estate taxes will have been repealed, the Fair Not Flat Tax is only a moderate departure from the status quo. In many ways it is simply a better version of the tax system we already have in place.

WINNERS AND LOSERS IN TRANSITION

OK, I'm sure a lot of you are thinking, it can't be that easy. I do believe that the Fair Not Flat Tax as a consistent spending tax is a simple and appealing concept. I also believe that because our inconsistent income tax already has features of a spending tax, the technical problems in transition will not be too great. Still, there will be political problems. Here I confess to seeing trouble. Change is never easy.

The media like to list who will win and who will lose under various tax reform plans. Newspapers and magazines crank out tables showing how typical households would fare under different options being considered. These tables are all too often the beginning and end of debate. Once a group of people have been stamped as "losers" on the front page, it is awfully difficult to get them to listen further. Nobody likes to lose anything, especially money.

There is, of course, nothing wrong with people's concern about their financial situation. It's human nature to care about one's own pocketbook. A tax reform plan that doesn't take this natural tendency into account is doomed to failure. Fairness requires getting the distribution of benefits and burdens down right; this is why the rate structure is such an important part of tax. A plan with too many losers isn't going to get very far—and it shouldn't.

But the list of "losers" under a transition to the Fair Not Flat Tax is limited and shouldn't stand in the way of much-needed reform. Let's consider them one at a time.

Potential Losers

There are four categories of people who might lose out in a transition to the Fair Not Flat Tax.

TAX EXPERTS

One group consists of specialists and politicians who make their living off the current mess of a system: the former by doling out advice, the latter by doling out special interest tax breaks. These folks will be kept busy enough during the transition to the better tax, but once it is completed, many tax lawyers, accountants, and maybe even politicians will have to find another line of work (or committee to serve on). But we can hope—and expect—that anyone clever enough to figure out tax today will be able to find better and more rewarding things to do in the future, and that we'll all be better off for the change.

SPECIAL INTERESTS

A second group of potential losers need not be losers at all: farmers, real estate professionals, charities, municipalities and the holders of their tax-free bonds, and other special interests that are helped under the current system. In regard to all such groups a basic fact should guide us through:

Any special interest helped under the income tax can be helped under any comprehensive tax system, including the Fair Not Flat Tax.

We can allow deductions or other special provisions to help these or other causes, just as we do now under the income tax. Under a consistent spending tax, though, we will all at last—and at least—be able to understand what it is we are doing. It will be harder for politicians to enact secret, hidden tax deals for special interests for bad reasons. The question with any particular claim for "special" treatment will be whether the associated use of wealth represents a fair exception from the general pattern of taxing spending. Emergency medical services, for example, might best be thought of as a necessity for which no one should be taxed regardless of income level, so we could allow a deduction under the Fair Not Flat Tax for medical expenses. Other claims will be more dubious. It's all simple and fair.

RICH SPENDERS

The third category of losers in the shift to the Fair Not Flat Tax will come from the ranks of the rich. Importantly, not all of the wealthy will lose: indeed, many wealthy people will be counted among the winners. Who's who—that is, who will win and who will lose? In short:

Rich savers will win, but rich spenders will lose.

This is as it should be—it's what the Fair Not Flat Tax aims to do. Wealthy savers are helping us all. Wealthy spenders are not. A major impetus behind the reform proposal is to reverse the pattern of current law that punishes ants and rewards grasshoppers. Any movement toward a better, fairer tax must undo those effects. Rich spenders like the fictional Artful Dodger will be losers in the transition because their taxes will increase. But they are only losing the unfair advantage they started with; we need shed few tears on their behalf.

CURRENT SAVERS

If we need not cry for the fate of rich big spenders, there is one group of Americans to whom we ought to pay more attention and respect.

These are people who have saved and paid taxes under today's inconsistent income tax, who might be taxed again in a general shift to a postpaid consumption, or spending, tax. Imagine Ant's reaction after going to spend the money in her already double-taxed bank savings account, only to learn that now a national spending tax is in place!

To the extent that current savers are elderly, and the spending money being taxed comes from their Social Security benefits, we could give larger rebates under the sales tax and exclude Social Security receipts from the supplemental spending tax. (This would remove today's unfairness of sometimes taxing Social Security benefits that relate to previously taxed wages.) Exempting Social Security benefits would limit the problem to those capital savings that have already been taxed under the inconsistent income tax. Of course, not all savings have been taxed under the current system: indeed, most have not. For those that have been taxed, a technical feature of the status quo can come in handy as we make the transition. Current savers have basis—after-tax dollars by definition—in their investment assets. The problem becomes what to do about preenactment basis, basis that is hanging around in a system that no longer needs it.

There are two major lines of thought about what we should do. One, many economists believe that we ought to do nothing at all. This is the efficient approach, because preenactment basis represents a "sunk cost"—it's water under the bridge. Simply ignoring preenactment basis and running the risk of doubly taxing some savers would not distort any new or future economic decisions. Simplicity and efficiency suggest going cold turkey in the move to the Fair Not Flat Tax.

But something strikes me as unfair about that answer. And so, two, there are steps we can take to avoid subjecting old savings to another round of tax. The main mechanism for saving under the Fair Not Flat Tax is the Trust Account. In the transition to the new tax, there will be a period during which taxpayers can transfer their existing savings into Trust Accounts. We can have some kind of carrot-and-stick incentive system to make sure that taxpayers do this. A plausible stick is that taxpayers will be taxed on the sale of assets not transferred into a Trust Account. A plausible carrot is that taxpayers would get some kind of credit or deduction for the preenactment basis of assets that are put into Trust Accounts in a timely fashion.

Under such a transitional plan, people who have saved and paid taxes on their savings under the current inconsistent income tax would get a bit of a break for the first few years under the Fair Not Flat Tax. This is a compromise, of course. It is not perfect, and it might be complex. But it would help ease the pain for one group of taxpayers who might legitimately evoke our sympathies.

Sure Winners

If tax professionals, special interests, rich spenders, and current savers are possible losers in the transition to the Fair Not Flat Tax, they pale in comparison to the sure winners: all the rest of us. Nearly every American will gain tremendously from the greater simplification and understandability of the new tax system. The ability finally to collect some tax from rich spenders ought to help lower the tax rates facing ordinary consumers. All Americans will henceforth be able to save without fear of immediate taxation, to develop the savings habit and sow the seeds of future economic betterment. Whereas rich spenders like Artful Dodger and the prodigal Lear daughters will be losers under the new regime, rich savers like King Lear and his noble Cordelia will be winners. No longer will high-end savers fear the complex and contorted traps of double taxation under an income tax, nor will they lie in dread that the tax collector will dance on their graves.

While certain rich savers will win by repeal of the death tax, their good fortune will inure to the benefit of all. When the wealthy save, they help society. A tax system that leads rich dads to mock their poor fellow citizens while living large tax free will have been stood on its head: we will have a model in place that can lead to class teamwork, not class conflict.

These are pretty nice gains to tally on the positive side of the case for change.

TECHNICAL ISSUES

There are some technical issues involved in the transition to a consistent spending tax. I have left most of them aside or have treated them in the Questions and Comments section. A few of the sources I discuss in the bibliographic notes at the end of the book provide more extensive discussions of transitional concerns. I have come to believe, however, that the potential for transitional problems is usually greatly exaggerated. Most academic discussions of transitions assume that what we have now is an income tax. We don't. We have an inconsistent income tax with many characteristics of a consumption tax. That renders the case for going through the transition to a consistent spending tax more compelling and the transition itself less onerous.

A technical issue I just considered is the problem of preenactment basis, which affects savers—the noble ants whom we may not want to tax twice. I described ways to deal with this problem. But a related problem exists on the flip side, that of the ignoble grasshoppers. Here we face the risk that carefree spenders will go on a grand binge, borrowing and spending away before the Fair Not Flat Tax takes effect because they know that the new tax will fall on debt-financed consumption. Understanding the root cause suggests a possible solution: we could deny a deduction for the repayment of preenactment debt, thus limiting the ability of Artful Dodger to borrow and spend before the Fair Not Flat Tax comes into full flower.

And so on down the line: the consistent principles of the Fair Not Flat Tax can be counted on to answer the most technical of objections. There will be work for the experts to do in crafting the best answers. But this work can, and should, be done.

THE TIME IS RIGHT

At the dawn of the twenty-first century, there is for the first time in our public imaginations the possibility of a large surplus in the federal budget. Liberals would use this money for more social spending. Conservatives would use it for more tax cutting. I say that the surplus gives us an opportunity to catch up on some long-deferred maintenance in our social and legal lives, an opportunity to finance the transition to a better, fairer, more sensible tax system.

Tax reform doesn't have to be about tax reduction. We can strive to make the move toward the Fair Not Flat Tax as revenue neutral as possible. Because the ultimate prize is a tax system that is sensible and fair, we should certainly consider providing transitional relief to prevent some constituencies from losing out and therefore opposing change. The surplus gives us much-needed room to maneuver. The lingering disaster of a tax system generates the urgency to try. The time is right to get tax right. Let's do it.

Toward Class Teamwork,
Not Class Conflict

People think taxation is a terribly mundane subject. But what makes it fascinating is that taxation, in reality, is life. If you know the position a person takes on taxes, you can tell their whole philosophy. The tax code, once you get to know it, embodies all the essence of life: greed, politics, power, goodness, charity. Everything's in there. That's why it's so hard to get a simplified tax code. Life just isn't simple.

—Former IRS Commissioner Sheldon Cohen, quoted in Jeffrey H. Birnbaum and Alan S. Murray, *Showdown at Gucci Gulf*

THESE ARE INTERESTING, HOPEFUL, YET PRECARIOUS TIMES in America. Notwithstanding the occasional market downturn, the U.S. economy is flourishing—we're the richest nation in the history of nations. But our wealth is not evenly spread. Our rich are getting richer, often unburdened by taxation altogether. Yet most ordinary Americans are working harder than ever just to get by, highly burdened by taxation on all sides. This is not a fair or stable situation; it's a situation that's ripe for class conflict.

It doesn't have to be this way. We can fix our tax system and put all Americans—rich and poor—on the same side. We can have a social and economic model built on class collaboration, not class confrontation.

This book is about tax, but tax, as Sheldon Cohen suggests, is about life. Tax shapes how we live and who we are. Tax today is part of the tension between economic classes, but it could help to bridge the divide. Getting our tax system right can improve our economy, our politics, and ultimately and most importantly, ourselves.

IMPROVING OUR ECONOMY

A bad tax system makes for economic waste. The current disgrace of a tax system is a drain on our national economy. Conservatives often argue that the size of the federal government is the real problem, but there's a lot to be said for the public goods and services that government provides, and someone has to pay for them. No matter the size of the public sector, our current tax system foolishly distorts economic decisions and crimps economic growth. The time, money, and other resources that this great nation devotes to complying with and trying to beat the tax system are a major part of the problem. The losses are large.

The Fair Not Flat Tax is a better, more consistent, more principled tax than what we have today. It distorts neither decisions about how much to save nor decisions about the form of savings. Capital is good for us all, and the Fair Not Flat Tax releases capital from the perverse investment incentives of the status quo. A better tax system can and should make ours a wealthier, happier nation. It's about time.

IMPROVING OUR POLITICS

A bad tax system makes for bad politics. This is perhaps the biggest flaw in the status quo. The present tax system is so complicated and unprincipled that the public abstains from any detailed consideration of it. The system encourages and enables complex hidden deals between politicians and special interests. This corrupts our politics and prevents us from looking into other reforms to make our society fairer. Lobbyists pour tons of money into Washington trying to get special tax breaks. So long as they get these deals and get away with it, people will keep pouring in the dollars. Our politics will remain corrupt and dominated by money.

In its basic principles the Fair Not Flat Tax is simpler and more transparent than our present tax. There will be no need for special savings provisions. Because the tax will fall consistently on private spending, the only question in examining various claims for deductions and credits is whether a particular use deserves special treatment. That's a decision that the media and individual citizens can help to monitor far better than they can watch over the inconsistent income tax.

Making the tax system simpler and more transparent might go a long way toward changing the woeful state of business as usual in Washington. That's an important goal, and it's worth a try. It's about time.

IMPROVING OURSELVES

Important as our politics and our economy are, there is an even greater reason to get tax right. Tax affects who we are, how we live. A bad tax system, left unchecked, can lead to a bad citizenry. That's the real fear for tax today.

A huge and pervasively coercive system like tax cannot help but influence what kinds of people we are and might reasonably hope to become. The present inconsistent income tax encourages an odd personal psychology. It punishes ants and the millionaires next door, and it suggests that we all become grasshoppers and die-brokers. This is far out of step with the basic American values that have made this country what it is.

Of course, as we have learned, our income tax system doesn't work in practice the way it is supposed to work in theory. The inconsistent income tax we have is even worse than a consistent income tax would be. Tax in America today is a confused and confusing mixture of various tax systems that allows rich and clever people like Rich Dad to pay no taxes whatsoever. Heirs like Lear's Goneril and Regan can acquire massive wealth early in their lives and spend away without ever paying any tax. The whole system is set up against work and ordinary middle-class forms of savings and in favor of overconsumption, manipulation, and deceit. The rich, clever, and well-advised win. The not-rich lose. If tax—this large and coercive instrument of state control—is not principled, its effects on us cannot be principled either.

THE BATTLE OF THE BEST-SELLERS, REDUX

Just as the fictional Ant and Grasshopper have battled it out in this book, so have two groups of people drawn from popular contemporary books: the millionaires next door and the die-brokers. Under today's disaster of a tax system the former are the big losers, and the latter the big winners. The Fair Not Flat Tax turns this bit of absurdity on its head.

High savers like the typical millionaire next door help us all with their hard work and thrift. Then we thank them today with a potentially triple tax and wonder why so many resort to complex planning schemes to avoid it. Meanwhile financial planners advise us to die broke, suggesting that we're foolish if we don't.

The Fair Not Flat Tax leaves millionaires next door alone, preferring to go after the spenders among their heirs. There is nothing wrong and a good deal right with working hard, living prudently, and saving well. If this means that some people will die rich, so be it. For if everyone starts taking the best-selling advice to die broke, then we as a society we will be forced to live poor. If we allow some of our best, brightest, and most productive economic actors to die rich, we can all live better. Why not? It's sensible. And it's fair.

The Fair Not Flat Tax is motivated by a quest for principle and fairness. It rests on two consistent ideals drawn from core American values:

- We should tax spending, not work or savings.
- Spending on luxuries can and should bear a higher tax rate than spending on ordinaries, which in turn can and should bear a higher rate of tax than spending on necessities.

This consistent, progressive spending tax brings the tax system in line with the best understanding of who we are and who we want to be. It listens to both the conservative opposition to taxing capital and the liberal case for moderate progressivity in our major national tax. Most of all, it listens to the people, who yearn for something simpler, more efficient, fairer, and more understandable than the mess of a tax system we now have.

The Fair Not Flat Tax does not encourage conspicuous consumption on one hand and discourage savings on the other. It tries instead to clamp down a bit on luxury fever, in all of our best interest. The Fair Not Flat Tax assures that no one in America will have to pay tax on the very basics of life, and it only moderately and unobtrusively taxes the ordinary expenditures of the vast middle classes. The Fair Not Flat Tax stays out of decisions to save, and it no longer punishes—two or three times—certain thrifty but ill-advised taxpayers. By reversing course to tax spending, not work and savings, the Fair Not Flat Tax will allow us to provide better for our children's future. In so doing, it will provide better for us all.

Finally, the Fair Not Flat Tax will ask the nation's most fortunate people to join the team, not set themselves up against it. Only the handful of people fortunate enough to be spending large sums of money will have to fill out forms and pay the supplemental spending tax. The Fair Not Flat Tax will not excessively burden our richest, wealthiest citizens as long as they are working, saving, and living well but not lavishly. It will stay out of their savings and investment decisions; it will simply ask them to be better partners in our communal future.

That's all pretty good. It's far better than what we have now. It's fair. It's worth fighting for. It's about time.

QUESTIONS AND COMMENTS ON THE FAIR NOT FLAT TAX

This book covers a lot of ground, and most readers probably have many questions and comments by now. The following pages address what I expect to be the most common ones based on my years of experience in teaching, discussing, and writing about tax reform. Because I've surely missed some important concerns, I invite you to write or e-mail me with yours at emccaffe@law.usc.edu. I'll try to get back to you, and I'll include the most pressing new questions, comments, and objections in subsequent editions of this book.

FIRST THINGS FIRST: THE BASIC PRINCIPLES
OF THE FAIR NOT FLAT TAX

Before getting into more detailed matters, this part addresses the basic principles and structures of the Fair Not Flat Tax. Questions and comments here tend to fall into two broad groups, relating to the tax's base and its rate structure. "Why should we tax consumption?" people ask. "And why have progressive tax rates?" Here are some answers.

Why Should We Tax Consumption?

Are you sure it's wise to tax spending? Isn't consumption good? Isn't it the engine of our economy?

Yes. Consumption is good. It is indeed the engine of our economy. Consumption is also the most common measure of a person's well-being. How much we consume shows how well we live—and we all want to live well.

But that doesn't have much to do with the Fair Not Flat Tax. Although this is a consistent consumption tax, it is most definitely not an "anti-consumption" tax. It does not oppose consumption. Far from it.

First of all, understand that the Fair Not Flat Tax won't change the bottom line much for most Americans. Tax rates won't increase for any but the wealthiest spenders. For many lower- and middle-class Americans, tax rates will decrease, hopefully more and more over time as the greater efficiencies of the new system take hold. Most Americans will be able to consume *more* under the Fair Not Flat Tax—indeed, that is a large part of what makes it fair. The Fair Not Flat Tax aims to make life simpler and better for lower- and middle-class Americans.

Indeed, for the many Americans who do not save, the Fair Not Flat Tax doesn't change the tax base at all. When people consume everything they earn, an income and a consumption tax come down to the same thing. A consumption tax isn't opposed to consumption, any more than an income tax is opposed to income. The Fair Not Flat Tax rests on a simple principle: given that we have to tax something, sometime, spending is a better thing to tax than work or savings. For most Americans, the Fair Not Flat Tax will simply mean less paperwork, equal or lower taxes, and greater ease in saving what they are able to save; it will not mean less consumption.

If that's all true—if the Fair Not Flat Tax isn't a big change for most Americans—then why should we care?

We should care for several reasons. One, although the Fair Not Flat Tax doesn't mean much change in the *what* or *how much* of taxation for the overwhelming majority of Americans, it does represent an important change in the method or technique—the *how*—of taxing. Under the tax as I have sketched it out, most Americans will no longer have to fill out annual tax returns. The national sales tax or VAT will remove a major compliance burden from ordinary Americans. That's a huge change, and one that will make many citizens much happier.

Two, the Fair Not Flat Tax rests on a consistent principle that all Americans can understand and endorse: we should tax spending, not work or savings. This principle can serve as a guide to subsequent tax reform. It will help to make our politicians more accountable and our economy more efficient.

Three, the Fair Not Flat Tax does make a difference in how we tax the rich. Although we are talking only about a small percentage of Americans, this is an important group for the nation's overall saving and consumption patterns. Because there is a slight increase in the top tax rate in my admittedly rough proposal—families of four who spend over $1 million a year on themselves will now be in a 50 percent marginal tax rate bracket—and because all spending will now bear a tax (no more Tax Planning 101), there will be an added burden on consumption for these wealthy few. But in exchange, the Fair Not Flat Tax will drop altogether the estate tax and all other attempts to tax savings or capital directly. Rich spenders will see a tax increase, while rich savers will see a tax decrease and a much easier and far more efficient system.

Again, most of that affects only the wealthiest minority of Americans. But the behavior of the wealthiest Americans is extremely important to our economy and to our sense of community. A tax system that encourages the richest among us to consume and not to save is perverse. The Fair Not Flat Tax does the opposite. By encouraging the rich to save—and to save over the long term—it makes them better partners in the project of creating a better America.

Are savings really all that important?

Yes, savings are very important. The national pool of savings helps to keep interest rates low. This in turn helps today's homeowners, students, and middle-class consumers, as well as future generations— our children and our children's children. America discovered during the 1990s that a strong capital stock is vital to the nation's health. Government borrowing had depleted the country's pool of capital, so when the federal government finally reined in its runaway deficits, it helped to spur one of the longest sustained-growth periods in our nation's history. Saving is saving, whether done by the government (via paying down its debt, say) or by individuals. Increased private savings is a large part of the way the Fair Not Flat Tax can help the cause of middle- and lower-class consumption.

Here is a related point: consumption is good, but so is savings. And savings is nonconsumption. The basic idea of the Fair Not Flat Tax is to make it easier for the rich to save, and by definition this means making it harder for them to consume—because if we aren't taxing savings, we're only taxing consumption. There's no way around this bit of accounting logic.

What about the risk of oversaving?

America might have been oversaving in the 1930s, during the Great Depression, and other nations, such as Japan, might have had bouts of this "disease" since. Economists debate whether oversaving has ever occurred, but it is certainly possible in theory for a nation to save too much—or, equivalently, to consume too little. The key point is that America is certainly not oversaving now; currently almost all economists think that America is undersaving. We should save more—and that means we should consume less.

But here is a very important point, often misunderstood: if we ever did find ourselves saving too much under a consistent consumption tax such as the Fair Not Flat Tax, we wouldn't have to start taxing savings again to reverse course. We could instead set ourselves right by taking advantage of the excess capital stock to lighten the tax on consumption. Lowering tax rates would be like having a sale of sales: "All consumer spending 10% off!" We would expect to see more consumption and less savings under the lower tax rates. We could also boost public spending—on health, education, or the general welfare, for example—although this Keynesian solution to the problem of oversaving and underconsumption is somewhat out of favor right now.

Don't people disagree about the importance of the nation's pool of savings?

Of course. People have reasonable disagreements about many, perhaps most, tax and economic matters. But here's the critically important point for the Fair Not Flat Tax: even if savings were not important, we should still have a consistent consumption tax, something like the Fair Not Flat Tax. The case for such a tax is logically independent of preferences about the ideal size of the nation's capital stock or savings level. Increasing the nation's pool of savings is only one reason for moving to a consumption tax. It is not even the most important reason. The main reason to adopt a consistent consumption tax is that the inconsistent income tax has been a disgraceful failure, a complicated mess that is neither efficient nor fair.

A consistent consumption tax is far simpler than the current inconsistent income tax both in theory and in practice. Most important, a consistent consumption tax is fairer—especially to those middle-class Americans who are trying to save. So there are very compelling reasons to have such a tax even if we calibrate tax rates so as to keep the total amount of national savings constant.

So why do people so commonly object that a progressive consumption tax plan is anti-consumption?

That's a good question, one that gets to the very important psychological dimensions of tax, about which I haven't said much in this book. People don't like to be taxed, of course. Whenever they hear of a tax proposal, they immediately try to figure out what it means for them and for their pocketbooks. If they suspect that their taxes will go up—or will not go down as much as they would like them to do—arguments against the proposal follow. That's human nature.

The interesting thing is that almost all of the people who object to a progressive consumption tax because "consumption is good" don't really oppose taxing consumption: they are usually the very same people who object to the taxation of savings under an income tax. These folks want to see the capital gains tax lowered or the gift and estate tax repealed. They love the flat-tax proposals, which, as we have seen, are all flat consumption taxes—no one objects to the common flat-tax plans by saying "consumption is good." The problem is that we cannot have it both ways. If we don't tax savings, we will have a consumption tax.

What this shows is that the real complaint is not that "consumption is good," but rather that "all consumption—including that of rich people—is equally good." It's really an argument against the "progressive" part of the progressive consumption tax, not against the "consumption" part. Almost everyone likes consumption taxes; the rich just don't like progressive ones.

It sounds like there is a lot of confusion in the talk of tax.

Exactly. People are getting their messages mixed up. There are three agendas at work in talk of tax today, and they are often commingled.

One agenda is to cut taxes, to downsize government. I've generally left that one alone. I've recommended a tax reform plan that is broadly revenue neutral; it would have no direct effect on the size of the tax system, although the simple, rounded numbers I have used may actually be a bit too low for current government needs.

The second agenda is to change the distribution of taxes—to flatten them so the rich will pay proportionately less. But if we kept revenue constant and lowered rates on the rich, we'd have to increase rates on the middle- and lower-income classes. I have argued at length that such a change wouldn't be fair. The Fair Not Flat Tax is roughly distributionally neutral: it doesn't significantly change the broad pattern of who bears the tax burden.

The third agenda is what the Fair Not Flat Tax plan is about: getting a fair and principled form for our tax system. I believe that if we focus on this goal alone in an open-minded way, we can see that broad, bipartisan consensus is possible on a consistent consumption tax. If we adopt such a tax while keeping the total amount of taxes and their distribution more or less constant, we will necessarily have a progressive consumption tax.

But if we're going to have a consumption tax, how are we ever going to define consumption? Won't that be complex?

It would indeed be complex to list all the items that make up consumption. But the Fair Not Flat Tax doesn't have to do anything of the sort. It doesn't have to list every item of consumption any more than an income tax does. The basic definition, Income = Consumption + Savings, is a truism. It tells us that all money is either spent or not. Similarly, we can define consumption with reference to income and savings. Specifically, Consumption = Income − Savings.

Under the Fair Not Flat Tax, we define income pretty much as always: wages and inflows from investments (the latter now meaning withdrawals from Trust Accounts), plus net borrowing. Then all we have to do is define savings. The Fair Not Flat Tax does that simply enough by referring to contributions to Trust Accounts and repayment of debt. The result, income minus savings, is consumption. Voilà. We have defined consumption—all money available for spending that is not saved—without attempting the tedious task of adding up items of consumption one by one. The Fair Not Flat Tax is thus a general tax. Its definition of taxable consumption doesn't depend on identifying each and every object of consumption.

Why Progressivity?

Wouldn't a flat tax be fairer than a progressive tax?

Many conservatives have convinced themselves that flat, and only flat, is fair. As I've noted at several points, there is no way to prove that a progressive tax is fairer than a flat one, but here are some compelling arguments in favor of some rate progression in the basic tax system:

- All of the common flat-tax plans include a zero bracket or exemption level for low-end consumption, so they are in reality two-rate plans. The principled logic behind such proposals is that minimal, low-end levels of income or consumption should bear a lower rate of tax than ordinary levels should. But once we have decided on that principle, why stop there? Why not include additional brackets to reflect our reasonable social judgment that high-end consumption should bear a higher rate of tax than ordinary consumption? That's what the Fair Not Flat Tax does.

- A genuine flat-tax plan would mean that tax increases on the vast middle class would help pay for tax reductions for the rich. But it's unfair to expect the middle class to pay for tax reform—they're paying enough under our tax system as it is.
- The preceding point is all the more compelling because the rich will benefit most from the repeal of the gift and estate tax and the systematic nontaxation of savings under the Fair Not Flat Tax. The new tax represents a grand compromise: a concession to traditional conservatives on the tax base, and a concession to traditional liberals on the tax rate. It's all fair.
- Getting the *what* of taxation right changes the nature of the debate over the *how much* question. The case for a consistent progressive consumption tax turns on the idea that luxurious or high-end spending can and should bear a higher marginal tax rate than ordinary spending, which should in turn bear a higher marginal rate than low-end spending. That's a principled case. A logical flip-side to this argument is that no one should be forced to pay high marginal tax rates: such high burdens should depend on people's choices to spend or not. A progressive spending tax is voluntary in an important sense.
- Some rate progression in the major comprehensive federal tax is needed to offset regression in other taxes, such as payroll taxes, state and local sales taxes, and, most likely, business taxes.
- The wealthy receive more of the benefits of an advanced democracy like the United States, and so it is appropriate to ask them to pay a bit more at the margin to help finance public goods, such as national defense, roads, education, and environmental protection.
- The wealthy can more easily afford to pay a higher tax rate; a moderate degree of progression actually effects an equal sacrifice from all citizens. And the Fair Not Flat Tax gives the wealthy an important choice in how to help out the broader community: through their continued savings or by paying a tax to the government on their high-end personal spending.
- The bottom line is that the American people, in polls and in

practice, have long supported a moderate degree of progression in tax burdens, and they seem highly unlikely to support a flat tax that involves a tax increase on the many to pay for a tax decrease for the few. The people deserve the last word. Tax reform should not be held hostage to conservative insistence on tax reduction for the rich.

That all doesn't decisively answer the objection that flat is fair. Nor does chapter 5, where I discuss progressivity at length. Life is like that: some debates never end. But at least we can have a friendly discussion about what is fair and leave it up to the people to decide in the end.

What gives the government the right to take more from a rich person? Isn't that just playing Robin Hood?

This fairly common objection is another variant of the criticism of progressivity. There are lots of arguments against progressive tax rates, many of them masquerading as arguments against something else. Conservatives can be passionate in their dislike of progressivity and persistent in their criticisms of it, notwithstanding the deep popular support for moderate progressivity in American taxes.

So I'll rest my case on what I have already said: the Fair Not Flat Tax isn't all that progressive—it is certainly no more progressive than what we've seen in prior periods of American history—and it's designed at least in part to counter regressive taxes elsewhere. It also doesn't just "take from the rich." It waits to see if, when, and how the wealthy spend their money, then extracts what is essentially a progressive sales tax on these voluntary decisions.

You just noted that business taxes are "most likely" regressive. What does this mean, and what would the Fair Not Flat Tax do about such taxes?

The Fair Not Flat Tax as I have sketched it out doesn't call for eliminating or reducing business taxes, but there are good reasons to consider doing so. These reasons start with the common-sense principle that businesses don't really pay taxes, people do. Because a business is a fictional legal entity, the dollars it pays to the government ultimately must come from flesh-and-blood humans' pockets. Economists aren't sure who really pays business taxes in the end—some think that they fall on workers, others on consumers, and still others on investors generally. In any event, the taxes are distorting and inefficient, and their claims to fairness are badly undercut by the uncertainty about who ultimately bears their burden.

So although I haven't addressed business taxes in this book, there is a good case for eliminating them. Several popular tax reform proposals call for doing just that. But business taxes are now in place, provide a significant amount of revenue, and are popular. Although there is much to be said for keeping business tax rates low, and perhaps looking to their long-term, gradual elimination, this might best await the next great American tax revolt.

Hasn't history proven that high tax rates hurt us all by discouraging productive growth and investment?

Yes, I do think that this has pretty much been proven. This is why my proposed rates under the Fair Not Flat Tax are not too high, certainly not by historic standards. The highest level of the supplemental personal consumption tax added on to the 10 percent national sales tax or VAT generates a top marginal tax rate of 50 percent on a very tiny fraction of truly high-end spenders. That rate is far below the historic high of 94 percent, and it's not much above today's (as I write this) top marginal income tax rate of 40 percent.

Remember also that these rates would fall only on spending—on the personal decision to consume. The Fair Not Flat Tax repeals the gift and estate tax and systematically exempts savings from direct taxation. Recall that millionaires next door whose wealth falls within today's estate tax range face an effective tax on additional work and savings in excess of 70 percent, because they get hit first by the income tax's 40 percent rate, then later by the death tax's 55 percent one. Taxes on people who save will fall dramatically under the Fair Not Flat Tax. Wealthy people who are content to live on less than $1 million a year of personal spending will never have to confront the 50 percent bracket—they will see at most the same 40 percent bracket they are in now, and they will enjoy a more systematic exclusion for their savings to boot. I don't think that the Fair Not Flat Tax as proposed would be detrimental at all to the national economy.

But why would anybody ever work and save knowing that a progressive consumption tax would one day affect them?

This sophisticated objection rests on the assumption that people will reason backward, thinking something like: "I work in order to spend. But this progressive spending tax will make it harder to spend. So I'll stay home from the start." Fortunately, we can meet this sophisticated objection with some simple responses. First of all, even if this were an accurate description of how many of us think, then the work disincentives under the Fair Not Flat Tax wouldn't be much different from those under the inconsistent income tax. More important, this objection rests on an unrealistic view of the typical wealthy American's psyche. People do not work solely in order to spend money on themselves. Studies and common sense consistently reveal that people save for many reasons, including to be able to pass on wealth to their heirs. The Fair Not Flat Tax rests on a more plausible understanding of how most wealthy Americans think. A person earning a high income—in excess of $100,000 a year, say—might reason along the following lines:

I'm fortunate to be making so much money. I'll keep working hard and I'll live pretty well for myself and my family. But I will also save a lot in my Trust Account because it will ensure my financial independence. It will be there for emergencies or for when I need a lot of money—like when the kids go off to college. The wealth will also provide a fund for my retirement. If I keep being lucky and the account builds up and up, I'll give some of it to charity and leave some of it to my children and grandchildren when my spouse and I pass away.

If enough wealthy people think like that—as *The Millionaire Next Door* suggests that they do—they won't be deterred by relatively high tax rates on high levels of personal consumption. The person I've just imagined never plans on spending a whole lot of money on himself or herself in one short time period.

What about people who only want to spend their earnings on themselves? Won't they be deterred?

Yes: the people most deterred under the Fair Not Flat Tax will be those rich people who insist on spending all of their money on themselves and dying broke. Rich people who are willing and even happy to save will not be deterred. But I don't think that this pattern of incentives is a bad thing. In fact, I think that it's fair.

What if the predictions about work and savings behavior turn out to be wrong?

I stress that the case for the Fair Not Flat Tax does not rest on any narrow set of assumptions about work or savings behavior. The main motivation behind the tax reform plan is to get a fairer, more principled tax system in place. This is not a supply-side argument that depends on predictions that there will be more money for us all, that we will have a higher GDP, or anything like that.

I do believe that a solid majority of economists would agree with me that the Fair Not Flat Tax would improve the overall economy, at least over time, for several reasons. An income tax is generally inefficient because it is set against savings; our inconsistent income tax is so complicated and distorting that it is a particular disaster. A simpler, more principled consumption tax will be far more efficient, because it will interfere less with important decisions about work, savings, and investment. Thus, the collective pie should grow under the Fair Not Flat Tax. But that is still not the foundation on which the case for the Fair Not Flat Tax rests. Even if everything else stayed the same, the Fair Not Flat Tax would be more principled, more consistent, more sensible, and—most importantly—more fair than the complicated mess of a tax system we have now. That's a worthy goal all by itself.

Because the poor consume more of their income than do the rich, isn't a consumption tax regressive and unfair?

No. There are many popular misconceptions about tax, and this common objection relates to two of them, that all consumption taxes are flat and that they are all regressive. But consumption taxes need not be flat taxes, and, largely for that reason, they need not be regressive.

The rich do save more than the not-rich. This necessarily means that the not-rich consume a higher percentage of their income than the rich do. So it is true that the base of a consumption tax forms a larger percentage of a not-rich person's income than it does of a rich person's income. But this does not mean that a consumption tax has to be regressive, for we can adjust tax rates accordingly. A consumption tax can be as progressive as we want it to be.

The Fair Not Flat Tax, for reasons I have argued at length, is only moderately progressive—its highest marginal rate is just 50 percent, and this falls only on annual personal consumption in excess of $1 million for a family of four. That's hardly a socialist plan. But it's also not a regressive one.

You've pointed out that the Social Security contribution system is a regressive tax. What would the Fair Not Flat Tax do about it?

The Fair Not Flat Tax proposal doesn't call for changing the Social Security system directly, but I do believe that this is something we should think about. Security Security and Medicare contributions make up the largest tax burden for most American taxpayers today, as we saw in chapter 1. Some tax reform plans would indeed replace the Social Security system. There is a good case to be made that this is fair, especially because of the way the Social Security tax fails to differentiate among taxpayers on the basis of family size and such, and because it falls on earnings, not spending. But repealing the Social Security tax would put massive revenue expectations on any new comprehensive tax, and we may not be prepared for such a radical step. It might be better to concentrate on making less sweeping changes to improve the fairness of our present Social Security system.

For now we can content ourselves with greater public education about tax and use the regressivity of the Social Security contribution as one of the arguments for more progressivity in the other major federal tax—hopefully, the Fair Not Flat Tax.

THE HARDER PART: DETAILS, DETAILS, DETAILS

Even if we can all agree that we should have a consistent progressive consumption, or spending, tax, there are still a lot of questions and concerns about what exactly this would mean. This part leaves the abstractions and returns to the devilish domain of details.

Exemptions and Deductions

The Fair Not Flat Tax can't be *that* simple. What about special items like food or medical expenses?

There will be some complexities, but we need not do anything as broad as carving out exceptions for food and other necessities. This is the reason for—and the beauty of—the rebate or zero-bracket technique. Under the Fair Not Flat Tax, the typical American family of four gets to spend $20,000 or so tax free. No family will be taxed on the very basics of life. We can set this exemption or zero bracket higher, and we would want to index it for inflation. The rebate does its duty without creating lots of exceptions that would narrow the tax's base and thus drive its rates up. The Fair Not Flat Tax remains pretty simple.

In addition to the general exemption level or zero bracket, what exceptions should the Fair Not Flat Tax allow as a matter of course?

Consider the deductions that exist today under the inconsistent income tax: those for extraordinary medical expenses, charitable contributions, and certain education related activities, for example. Each can continue under the Fair Not Flat Tax. Extraordinary medical expenses and charitable contributions strike us as the kinds of consumption we should not be taxing. Education is more debatable, but still a case can be made for allowing more generous education deductions. Under the Fair Not Flat Tax, we would argue that the overall level of spending on medical care and charitable contributions is not what matters, but rather that these are distinctions of kind, not degree. We could, that is, conclude that such uses of money should not be taxable regardless of one's total consumption or spending.

Of course, each claim for special treatment can be matched with a set of objections. Allowing medical expense deductions might interfere with people's incentive to get health insurance. Charitable contribution deductions might allow the rich to benefit their preferred charities too much for general tastes. Deductions for private education may strike us as an unfair benefit to the rich that deals a blow to the cause of public education.

We don't need to resolve these debates here and now. Note by the way that these issues already come up under the inconsistent income tax. By definition, income includes all consumption as well as all savings. An income tax has to decide what consumption to tax every bit as much as a consumption tax does. We are used to making these kinds of decisions, so the Fair Not Flat Tax will not add any complexity to our lives in this regard. Indeed, we can make the same types of decisions about deductions under the Fair Not Flat Tax with a clear set of principles to guide us: we'll have a better sense of what we are doing, and why.

What about deductions for business expenses?

Like any comprehensive tax, the Fair Not Flat Tax will need to allow deductions for general business expenses. If a business spends one dollar in the hopes of making two, more power to it—the government is a partner in the net profits of society, so it will want those profits to increase just as the business's owners will. The government should not micromanage private enterprise by scrutinizing business deductions too closely.

But a problem arises when people have fun on the job. What should we do about pleasurable events—golf outings, three-martini lunches—that occur in the course of doing business? The basic principle of the Fair Not Flat Tax is that consumption—personal spending—ought to be taxable. It wouldn't be fair if some taxpayers could get their fun at the workplace, with nontaxed dollars, while others had to do so away from work, with taxed ones.

This raises a host of difficult issues. But once again, they are no different from ones we have long faced under the income tax, which is also supposed to include personal consumption in the tax base. There are many laws about what is and is not deductible as a business expense. These laws can survive the transition to the Fair Not Flat Tax. There won't be any new complexity.

Speaking of business expenses, what about fringe benefits?

Again, this issue would look much like it does under current law. With the important exceptions of pension plan contributions and medical insurance, fringe benefits under today's income tax are generally taxable to the extent that they constitute personal consumption.

Pension plans, one of the two largest categories of tax-favored fringe benefits, are a form of savings, so under a consistent spending tax they should not be taxed, whether contributions are made by the employer or the employee. In fact, the Fair Not Flat Tax is far simpler in its treatment of retirement savings than what we have now. Many complicated income tax laws relating to pension plans can be repealed, because under the Fair Not Flat Tax individuals are unlimited in their ability to save tax free. Medical insurance, the other large category of fringe benefits, may also not be taxable if there is a general exclusion from the consistent consumption tax for medical goods and services—that's not a category we want to tax, for reasons of policy.

That takes care of the largest fringe benefits, and existing rules should be adequate to take care of the rest.

Interest and Debt

What about deductions for home mortgage interest and the like?

The Fair Not Flat Tax continues the deduction for home mortgage interest allowed under current law. In fact, any consistent postpaid consumption, or spending, tax will have a general deduction for all interest. Debt is taxed when, but only when, it is used to consume things. You are taxed when you borrow, unless you borrow to invest (in which case the inclusion of debt is offset by a subtraction for savings). You are not taxed again when you pay off your debts, and you are also not taxed on the interest you pay on them. All interest ought to be deductible, and certainly home mortgage interest will be.

So all repayments of debt, and all interest on debt, will be fully deductible?

Yes. In case this sounds odd, think again of how a sales tax works. When you borrow money on a credit card to buy something, you pay the sales tax when you buy the item. You don't pay again when you pay off your credit card balance, with or without interest. This is not just an analogy. Like a sales tax, the Fair Not Flat Tax is a spending tax.

As a practical matter, how will the proceeds of debt be taxed? What are the D-2s?

Under the Fair Not Flat Tax—as under any consistent consumption, or spending, tax—debt is taxable when it is incurred and used to purchase consumption items. We can tax it by counting debt as income under the basic income-minus-savings structure. If you borrow $10,000, we count that as an inflow. If you invest the money, you have an offsetting deduction under the unlimited allowance for savings. If you don't save or invest it, you have spent it—and you must therefore pay tax on it.

In fact, borrowing is really just a form of savings: negative savings, something that decreases your net worth. Repaying a debt is a form of savings, too; it builds up your net worth and so is positive savings. The Fair Not Flat Tax's treatment of borrowing follows from its treatment of savings: subtracting a negative (borrowing) means adding, and so on. You won't pay a double tax on these borrowed dollars, however, because you won't pay tax again when you repay the debt. You'll get a deduction for repayments of principal and interest. The national sales tax or VAT operating on the 10 percent bracket gets this right as a matter of course. You pay the sales tax when you purchase a consumer item with cash or with a credit card. You don't pay a tax again when you pay off your credit card balance.

Under the supplemental personal consumption tax, banks and credit card companies will simply tell the government how much you borrowed in a year. Banks now use 1099 forms to report the interest they pay you; these will be replaced by the S-2 forms that report how much you save. Financial companies will use D-2 forms (D for *debt*) to report your borrowing minus your payments of principal and interest. You end up paying tax on wages, plus debt, minus savings: W-2 + D-2 − S-2.

Won't calculating debt be complicated in the case of credit cards? Balances fluctuate so much.

No, it won't be very complicated. We can just look at your balance as of one point in time, say midnight on January 1. If you started the year with $2,000 in credit card debt and end it with $2,500 in debt, you have added $500 of debt—you've consumed an extra $500 on the credit card company's tab. So your D-2 will read $500. If, on the other hand, you started the year with a $2,000 balance and end it with a $1,000 one, you have, in essence, saved $1,000—that was money you did not use during the year to buy new things for yourself or your family; you paid tax on the underlying consumption in an earlier year. So your D-2 will show a negative $1,000.

Remember, too, that if we use a national sales tax or VAT for the lowest positive rate bracket, most of these refinements will affect only the wealthy minority paying the supplemental personal consumption tax. The sales tax will automatically get it right for the rest of us. We can tolerate a certain amount of complexity, especially when we know that only the few, the rich, and the well-advised will be directly concerned with it.

What about taxpayers who default and don't pay back their debts?

Discharge of debt will be a much simpler matter under a consistent consumption tax than it is under an income tax. If you borrow money and consume the proceeds, you pay tax at the time of consumption. If you don't repay the principal, you don't get the deduction for repayment of principal.

Housing and Other Consumer Durables

Aside from the mortgage interest deduction, will housing be treated just like it is now under the income tax?

Pretty much, although the Fair Not Flat Tax can actually go farther in encouraging home ownership than present law does, if we treat the building up of home equity as a form of savings. Buying a home involves consumption as well as savings; I'll address the consumption part in a moment. For now, a simple example may help clarify the idea of home ownership as savings.

Suppose Fred Flintstone bought a new home outright, for $100,000 cash. Viewing home ownership as an asset—home equity is one of the most important forms of savings for many Americans after all— the Fair Not Flat Tax would give Fred a deduction for the $100,000, just as if he had put the money into a Trust Account for any other form of savings.

Now suppose Fred instead borrows the $100,000 to purchase the home. In the year of the initial acquisition, Fred's D-2 will show "income" of $100,000 from the debt while his S-2 will show an equal deduction of $100,000 for buying the home. The net result is a wash—there is no net inclusion or deduction at this point ($100,000 − 100,000 = 0). This is as it ought to be when one borrows with one hand and purchases an asset with the other: there is no real saving and no increase in net worth in such cases. As Fred pays off the mortgage, however, both the interest and the principal payments will be deductible. They will show up as negative items (for repayments) on his D-2 forms. Again this is as it should be, for as Fred pays down his mortgage and builds up his home equity, his net wealth increases. This discussion reminds us that debt is negative savings: when you incur debt, you dissave; when you pay down debt, you save.

By making payments of principal deductible, the Fair Not Flat Tax treats the building up of home equity in the same way it treats any savings taking place inside a Trust Account—no tax is due up front. When the house is sold, the Fair Not Flat Tax will tax the proceeds unless they are rolled over into another home or into a Trust Account.

But if we don't tax money that is used to buy a home, won't that be a windfall for rich people who buy mansions?

If we thought that the above treatment of housing was somehow too generous, we could simply limit the deductions for home mortgage interest or principal for expensive homes. We actually do both of these things now under the inconsistent income tax. A homeowner can deduct mortgage interest only up to $1 million of underlying principal. Similarly, gain on the sale of a home in excess of $500,000 per married couple is taxed. Both of these provisions are ways that the law taxes the home consumption of the rich. We could maintain this type of treatment under the Fair Not Flat Tax on the theory that housing above a certain level represents the kind of luxury that ought to be taxed.

What about the consumption value of homes? What about renters?

These are excellent questions. A significant percentage of personal spending goes toward the consumption of housing. Renters pay directly—with presently after-tax (that is, nondeductible) dollars. Homeowners "pay" only indirectly—by investing in their residences and sacrificing the investment yield they could otherwise realize on that wealth. Both an income tax, which is meant to include all consumption within its base, and a consumption tax ought to tax both forms of housing expense—the direct payment of rent and the indirect, invisible consumption value of owner-occupied housing. Today's inconsistent income tax, however, includes only rent in its base; it makes no attempt to tax homeowners on their housing consumption. The Fair Not Flat Tax has the same problem.

We could fix the situation by taxing the housing consumption of homeowners. Of course, that's easier said than done: it's hard to figure out what exactly the consumption value of a home is. But it is possible to make a guess, as the law already does in some circumstances, such as when a married couple gets a divorce. Some countries—England is one—value housing more systematically. We could use local property tax rolls to get at a fair market value for each home and work from there.

But all of that would be complicated and confusing, so today's inconsistent income tax doesn't even try to tax the consumption value of owner-occupied housing. The Fair Not Flat Tax as I have proposed it follows suit, largely for practical reasons. Still, the Fair Not Flat Tax has some advantages over the status quo. If we don't include housing in the national sales tax or VAT, we can at least remove the disparity between renters and homeowners for the vast majority of Americans—families spending less than $80,000 a year on themselves. True, this would mean not taxing an important element of consumption, but perhaps we should regard ordinary levels of spending on housing like we might medical expenses: as a necessity that should not be taxed.

This would leave the complexities and possible inequities to the relative few subject to the supplemental personal consumption tax. There are technical adjustments we can make to level the playing field between these wealthier renters and homeowners, such as allowing a renter's deduction or attempting to include some measure of the consumption value of owner-occupied housing in the tax base. But I'll spare further details here: my objective in these discussions is not to solve highly technical problems once and for all. Rather, it is to illustrate what the problems are and that the structure of the Fair Not Flat Tax sets them in a context that at least makes principled solutions possible.

It's not just a problem for housing: Some consumer purchases, like cars, last for many years. Isn't it unfair to tax their purchase price all at once?

This is the interesting, somewhat technical question of consumer durables. It is connected to the question of houses. There are a couple of lines of thought about this.

Imagine that Wilma Flintstone bought a car for $20,000 in Year 1, and it was expected to last for five years. If we made no adjustments to the proposed tax, Wilma would pay a spending tax on the full $20,000 in the year of purchase, even though she would still have the car at the end of the year. To avoid that, we could allow a form of negative depreciation. We could say that Wilma should only pay tax on $4,000 of the car's value each year. We would give her a deduction of $16,000 in Year 1 so that the net taxable consumption for the car in that year would be $4,000 ($20,000 − 16,000), and then we would charge back $4,000 a year to her for the next four years until taxes on the full $20,000 had been paid.

This kind of treatment is the inverse of the way we treat depreciable investment assets today, under the inconsistent income tax. If a taxpayer buys a business asset for $20,000 that will last for five years, we force him to spread his deductions over time—to deduct $4,000 a year. (We wouldn't have to depreciate business assets under the Fair Not Flat Tax, because, like all consumption-based taxes, it would allow business expenses to be deducted immediately.) What we would be doing for Wilma is allowing her to include the consumption item over time. Allowing Wilma to pay tax on the depreciation alone, or $4,000, would put her in the same situation as if she had leased the car. Note that borrowing to buy the car over time would lead to a different result: the full $20,000 of borrowing would be taxable right away, and we would then ignore repayments of the principal over time— just like with any sales tax.

Still, it doesn't really matter all that much how Wilma pays for her car. By opting for a lease, the buyer gets to pay the spending tax over time instead of all at once, but then the lease payments are higher than the purchase price, to reflect the time deferral involved. The government shouldn't care too much about this kind of thing; we can let the market sort it all out. Much the same analysis applies to wealthy people who would be subject to the supplemental personal consumption tax. The problem of consumer durables may be one we need not solve.

The National Sales Tax or VAT

Can a national sales tax or VAT really work?

Yes, I think that a national sales tax or VAT is realistic, especially at the moderate 10 percent level I have proposed. Many countries have similar taxes, and of course we have much experience with sales taxes at the state and local level. There is ample precedent to draw on and plenty of reason to be optimistic that problems with a sales tax or VAT can be worked out at least as well as problems are being worked out under today's inconsistent income tax.

Putting a national sales tax or VAT in place won't be easy, of course. Nothing of such magnitude ever is. There are definitely compliance issues—sales tax abuse is common around the world. All of this gives reason to start small. Many think tanks and other organizations are at work today on the question of how to implement a national sales tax or VAT; I refer to some of their work in the bibliographic notes. The problems posed are solvable.

On the other hand, I stress that replacing the lower brackets of the Fair Not Flat Tax with a national sales tax or VAT plus a rebate is an optional step. This simplifying move is possible because of the logical equivalence of a sales tax or VAT and any other form of a consistent postpaid consumption tax. Some people might prefer that certain features of the existing system be retained; they may think it good that more, not fewer, taxpayers fill out forms and therefore have more direct encounters with the tax system. So we might not want to take the step of including the national sales tax or VAT after all. Whether we do or not, the Fair Not Flat Tax is a much simpler, fairer, and more logically consistent tax system than the inconsistent income-plus-estate-tax mess we have now.

How would services be taxed under a sales tax or VAT?

Experts have been looking into this important question. The U.S. economy is now highly oriented toward services. A failure to include them in the national sales tax would drastically narrow the tax base, and rates would have to go up on those things that would be covered. This would be inefficient, complicated, and unfair. The good news is that plausible proposals exist for taxing services, and these have been tried in various states and nations. The problem of taxing services probably tilts the case in favor of a VAT instead of a national sales tax, but this is a matter that the experts can help to work out under the clear and consistent mandate of the Fair Not Flat Tax.

Should we have exceptions for food and other necessities under a national sales tax or VAT?

Generally we would not need to do so, because this is essentially what the rebate mechanism does, by defining necessities by level, not kind, of expenditure.

In case it still sounds a bit harsh to tax expenditures on food, note that this is what we already do under the inconsistent income tax. When you buy food, you do so with money that has already been taxed by the income tax system. There is no general deduction for food or other necessities under the income tax. The concern with fairness is taken into account by having a large zero bracket or exemption level that means that a family is not paying any tax at all on its first $20,000 or so of consumption.

The remaining questions about taxing necessities concern what kinds of expenses should be exempted regardless of a family's total spending level. There are some services—like medical services, for example—that we might think of as necessities at all levels of spending. The arguments for exempting a particular *kind* of expense from the national sales tax or VAT parallel the arguments discussed above for allowing a deduction under the supplemental personal consumption tax.

What about taxing sales over the Internet and other new or unusual forms of commerce?

A national sales tax actually has considerable advantages over state and local sales taxes in getting at electronic and other emergent forms of commerce. First of all, there is today an incentive to move businesses to places that have no sales tax. That's why many mail order businesses have moved to states like South Dakota. The Internet poses a threat to state and local sales tax revenues because it is often difficult to figure out where sales take place, and sellers can keep moving to avoid being taxed. Congress passed a law in the late 1990s exempting Internet sales from new state or local sales taxes for three years, and it seems likely to extend this period. If the moratorium period should end, we will have to face the issue directly: which states should collect what taxes? This could become a big problem as e-commerce grows more popular, taking business away from traditional stores. The federal government has a large advantage here: it can insist that the national sales tax or VAT be levied on all sales made to Americans, wherever they might live.

What about imports and exports?

Advocates of a national sales tax and of various forms of VAT have technical debates about whether the taxes should be "border adjustable." A national sales tax falls only on consumption within the country, so exports would bear no U.S. tax. A VAT, on the other hand, is imposed gradually throughout the production process. A teapot made in this country will have a VAT from the interim production processes built into its price, whether it is exported or not. Many advocates of a VAT therefore urge that the tax should be border adjustable, meaning that we should give exporters a credit for the VAT before they export their products. Others say that this is not necessary. I tend to agree that we should make the adjustment and let other forms of taxation, if any, deal with matters of international trade. Once again, these technical issues can be resolved by experts who are working under the direction of the clear and consistent mandate of the Fair Not Flat Tax.

The Rebate

If we do have a national sales tax or VAT, how would the rebate work?

The rebate gives every American relief from the national sales tax or VAT that forms the 10 percent bracket of the Fair Not Flat Tax. In essence, it creates a zero bracket. Say we wanted to give every American a $5,000 zero bracket. A family of four would get a $2,000 rebate, corresponding to 10 percent of $20,000. The family wouldn't be paying any net tax on its first $20,000 of consumption.

There are several ways to administer the rebate, and each would yield the same result. We could mail each American individual or family a check, make gradual deposits into bank accounts, or give credits built into paychecks—a form of negative withholding. We could achieve the same effect by simply allowing an exemption from Social Security and Medicare contributions, which act like a 15.3 percent flat tax when employer and employee shares are combined. If we told employers not to withhold 5 percent on the first $5,000 of each employee's earnings (adjusted for family size), and had them credit employees' paychecks with 5 percent of wages for the employer's share, too, we would pretty much be in the same place as if we mailed the rebate: taxpayers would get a 10 percent break on their first $5,000 of earnings. Employees could simply fill out a form listing the number of exemptions to which they are entitled, much like the W-4 forms that they complete today for purposes of calibrating wage withholding. Social Security numbers would have to be listed, and they could easily be checked to prevent double counting or other fraud. And so on.

If the rebate is administered through a wage-based system, what about people who don't have any earnings?

The three biggest categories of people who don't earn wages are poor people, who would be entitled to a rebate if we made it refundable (see the discussion below); children, who would receive their rebates through their parents' wages; and elderly people, whose rebates could be added onto their Social Security receipts. For any other categories of people without wages—wealthy capitalists, say—we could devise a solution easily enough. Such people might submit a form to the government listing the Social Security numbers of their family members and indicating the amount and sources of their nonwage income. We could then mail this relatively small number of people a rebate check.

Should the rebate be refundable?

A refundable rebate or credit is one that can bring a taxpayer's tax below zero: a family of four would get the full $2,000 rebate even if it didn't earn or spend $20,000. Both simplicity and fairness offer compelling reasons to have a refundable credit. It would make things simpler because we would not have to monitor paychecks to make sure that each American was in fact earning enough to warrant the full rebate amount. The credit could be administered simply by mailing every American a check for $500. A refundable credit would also be fair of course because families making so little money can use our help.

But precisely because there are many American families that make less than $5,000 per capita, a refundable rebate would be more costly than a nonrefundable one. This is why most proposals for a rebate mechanism involve a nonrefundable credit.

Under some tax plans the rebate would be phased out as income rises. Would the Fair Not Flat Tax do this?

Phaseouts are becoming increasingly common under the disaster of a tax system we now have: when an individual's earnings exceed a certain level of income, she loses a benefit conferred at an earlier range. One has to pay back the benefit, as it were. This simply means that there is a higher tax rate on earnings above that level. Phaseouts are rate increases achieved in a sneaky, hidden fashion. I am not a big fan of this technique.

Imagine that in Bedrock there is a 10 percent VAT with a rebate of $500 per person and a phaseout beginning at $50,000 of earnings. For every dollar Fred spent over $50,000, the Flintstones would have to give back the rebate they got on one dollar of Fred's first $20,000 in spending. If Fred spent $60,000, for example, the family would lose $1,000 of its rebate (10 percent of $10,000). By the time Fred spent $70,000, the family would have paid back all of the rebate for its first $20,000.

That would mean that over the phaseout range—from $50,000 to $70,000—the Flintstones would really be in a 20 percent tax bracket. They would continue to pay the 10 percent VAT as always, but they would also be losing ten cents out of every additional dollar, because they would be returning their $2,000 rebate. Losing money to the government means being taxed, no matter what we call it. So a phaseout just creates another tax bracket for the middle- and upper-income levels. I would prefer that we set up the rate structure openly and honestly and avoid the complications, unfairness, and deception of using phaseouts.

Accommodating Families

How does the Fair Not Flat Tax adjust for family size and so forth?

The simplest thing to do is to allow a $5,000 exemption per family member, defined under today's law to include spouses and children under eighteen. If we thought that this was too generous to larger families, we might limit the total number of exemptions per household to four, or lower the exemption for children, or allow a $5,000 exemption for the first two children and something less, like $2,000, for each additional one.

As a practical matter, Fred Flintstone would fill out a form listing the names and Social Security numbers of all of his dependents, just like he does on a W-4 form under current law. If Wilma also works, she will be able to claim her own exemption for the rebate; listing Social Security numbers will ensure that Fred and Wilma are not able to double count each other. We can adjust this basic structure any way we want to. We might give larger exemption levels to working adults (and hence larger ones to two-worker couples than to one-worker ones), for example, because working adults incur greater work-related expenses.

We could leave it at that—dealing with family matters in the rebate mechanism alone, even for wealthier families subject to the supplemental personal consumption tax. Or we could adjust the rate brackets for family size under the supplemental tax too. If a family of four would start paying the supplemental tax at $80,000, a family of six might have until $90,000, and so forth. In essence this would add on a $5,000 further exemption per family member. These basic principles are pretty much the same as those under today's inconsistent income tax.

Your first book, *Taxing Women*, addressed the problems that working women and two-earner families face under today's tax laws. Will the Fair Not Flat Tax do anything for them?

My concern in *Taxing Women* was to show the ways in which the American tax system is unfair to women, especially married working women with children, and to certain kinds of families, especially the increasingly common two-earner ones. These are some examples of the current tax system's embarrassing unfairness and inefficiency. The bias against women manifests itself in three ways:

- the system of joint filing, which aggregates husband and wife, putting the secondary earner at a rate bracket dictated by the primary earner's wages
- inadequate deductions for child care and other work-related costs of two-earner families
- the structure of the Social Security system, which has severe penalties against two-earner households built into it

The Fair Not Flat Tax can readily address all three problems within its structure. There would still be a bias against two-earner families if the Fair Not Flat Tax retained joint filing, because the second earner, almost always the wife, would be entering in a tax rate bracket dictated by the first earner's—almost always the husband's—salary. For most Americans this would mean that a wife would enter the workforce at a 10 percent rate, whereas the husband would get the benefit of the initial zero bracket. We may not see this so much under a national sales tax or VAT, but the effect is there nonetheless.

This gives us a reason to consider separate filing, especially under the supplemental personal consumption tax, but there are reasons we might not want to do that under a consistent spending tax. At the lower levels—for the lower and middle classes—we could give a working spouse a higher rebate than a nonworking spouse as a way to offset some of the additional costs of working. A working spouse might get a $10,000 exemption level, for example, whereas a nonworking one would get $5,000. This would in essence—and easily— create a system of separate filing for the overwhelming majority of two-earner American couples.

Two, a large part of the problem facing modern families and working wives today is that two-earner couples have to pay for child care, whereas one-earner families don't. The inconsistent income tax compounds the problem by having only very limited provisions for relief, meaning that two-earner couples have to pay for child care with after-tax dollars. We should make child care a service that is exempt from the national sales tax or VAT. This would be like giving everyone in the 10 percent bracket—the huge majority of two-earner couples—a full deduction for the costs of child care. Families in the supplemental personal consumption tax range would be paying tax on their child care at 10, 20, 30, or in very rare cases 40 percent—generally lower than current rates even without a fuller child care deduction.

Three, when fixing the Social Security system, we could give a secondary-earner exemption. This would eliminate the unfair practice of requiring working wives to pay the full tax with no corresponding increase in their benefits. Although this is a separate matter from the main subject of this book, it is part of the bigger project of making our tax laws fairer and more principled. As this brief discussion of the problems shows, however, we still have a long way to go in this regard.

Trust Accounts

What exactly would Trust Accounts be? How would they work?

A Trust Account would work just like a traditional IRA does now. Contributions to it entitle you to a deduction. The government more or less ignores what happens within the accounts as long as you invest in any of the many permissible ways that I will discuss shortly. You won't pay tax on investment yields and gains that stay in your account. You won't pay tax when you switch investments or sell an asset but keep the cash proceeds inside the account. There will be no such thing as basis in the assets. Only when you withdraw the money will you pay tax, and then at regular tax rates.

A Trust Account can be anything the law says it can be: a bank account, a stock brokerage account, real property, whatever. A taxpayer will simply have to register the account, by using her Social Security number and electing for the savings or investment vehicle to be designated as a Trust Account. That will authorize the account manager—the bank, mutual fund, or other entity—to report to the government net contributions and withdrawals each year. I suspect that most taxpayers will want to have a single large Trust Account held by their local bank or a major mutual fund company, but this isn't necessary. Just as taxpayers today can open new IRA accounts each year, they could easily have multiple Trust Accounts under the Fair Not Flat Tax. *Trust Account* is merely a label that the law will put on any tax-free savings vehicle.

How would people make gifts or pass on the Trust Accounts at death?

Easily. The Trust Account will simply be re-registered in another person's name and Social Security number. For example, Fred Flintstone could walk into a bank and say to the teller: "Please take $5,000 out of my account and place it in my daughter's." This transaction would be reported to the government as a transfer. Fred would pay no tax, and Pebbles would have the $5,000 in her own account. If and when she went to withdraw the money, she—and not her father—would be taxed on it.

What about assets that people have before the Fair Not Flat Tax goes into effect and that are not transferred into a Trust Account?

Here we encounter the complicated problem of preenactment basis, which I discuss briefly in chapter 6. We might keep the laws for the taxation of capital and savings on the books and apply them to assets not transferred into Trust Accounts. Because the Trust Accounts will generally be favorable to taxpayers, we'll hope that the problem of hidden assets won't be too severe and that it will fade over time. We could also apply penalties or fines to people who don't transfer their assets into Trust Accounts, or we could enlist financial intermediaries in the cause, requiring banks and other regulated financial institutions to register all of their accounts as Trust Accounts.

What about the lower- and middle-class people not subject to the supplemental personal consumption tax? Would they have Trust Accounts?

Most people live their whole lives and never consume more than $80,000 in any one year. They won't necessarily need Trust Accounts because they won't have to fill out the Fair Tax form or pay the supplemental personal consumption tax. They will simply collect their rebates and pay the national sales tax or VAT in the ordinary course of things.

Something of a problem might arise in the case of middle-class taxpayers who are able to save up large amounts by living frugally and then, when they are on the verge of being subject to the supplemental personal consumption tax, spend away. Or some taxpayers who suddenly enter a high-earning period might pretend to be saving some of their new salary by depositing previously accumulated wealth into a Trust Account. Say, for example, that Fred Flintstone has stashed away a few thousand dollars a year under his mattress and has built up a nice nest egg of $50,000. Suddenly, he gets a raise to $120,000 a year, so that his family falls in the supplemental tax range. Fred goes ahead and spends all $120,000 of his earnings, but then he takes the money out from under his mattress, puts it in a Trust Account, and takes a deduction. Fred is avoiding some of the supplemental spending tax he ought to be paying.

So understood, however, this is a fairly minor problem. It can be dealt with in the way that many problems are dealt with under the income tax today—through fines and penalties, audits, and so forth. As long as people breathe and governments tax, there will no doubt be some cases of tax abuse, and many more attempts at it. The Fair Not Flat Tax tries to minimize the opportunities for legitimate avoidance and to set up a principled structure for investigating and policing illegitimate avoidance. But it cannot promise that no abuse will occur.

The proposal calls for the government to oversee private Trust Accounts. Isn't this government meddling?

Well, it could be, of course, if it went too far. But there is nothing in the Fair Not Flat Tax to suggest that government regulation would or should be very intrusive.

The idea of regulating private savings might sound radical to many readers. It is not. Most capital in America is now regulated: savings held by banks, insurance companies, mutual funds, pension plans, large university and hospital endowments, charitable foundations. All of this need not be onerous. Relatively simple rules, such as those that now apply to IRAs, could apply to small and moderately sized Trust Accounts, perhaps those that hold up to $1 million. More complex rules could apply only to the handful of very large Trust Accounts held by the wealthiest people.

What rules do you recommend for preventing the misuse of wealth that accumulates in Trust Accounts?

These rules would fall into two broad categories. One set of rules would impose a loose diversification requirement on investments in the Trust Accounts. This would prevent the accounts from developing concentrated power within particular markets or industries. A second set of rules would prevent certain expenses—like lobbying costs and others that overly inure to the private benefit of the holder—from taking place inside the accounts. The individual freedom to lobby or run for office with tax-free dollars would be curtailed. Ross Perot would still be able to run for president, of course, but we simply would not allow his presidential run to be treated as a business expense or investment taking place inside a tax-favored Trust Account. We would treat Perot's run as we would any other kind of personal consumption, like taking a nice trip around the world. To run for president, Perot would have to withdraw money from his account and pay tax on it.

What would the Fair Not Flat Tax do about closely held and family businesses and the like?

This is an important question. We don't want to punish entrepreneurs for taking risks. Fortunately, it is a rather simple matter to carve out family businesses and to allow them to be held inside Trust Accounts.

Some readers no doubt noticed that I did not discuss farms or family businesses in chapter 4, where I argued against the current—and all possible—death taxes. The omission was deliberate. Nothing in my argument against death taxes turns on the *form* of the unspent wealth. Under the estate tax, "carve-outs" for family businesses are exceptions to the tax itself, and various manipulative games and avoidance techniques make them inefficient and unfair. Such carve-outs for family businesses under the estate tax are not a good idea, in part because the owner of a family business is no more noble or worthy a saver than an individual holding onto a portfolio of stocks and bonds.

Allowing closely held or family businesses to be held within the Trust Accounts, in contrast, is an exception not to the tax itself but to the regulatory requirements on the Trust Accounts, especially as regards their diversification. This is an altogether different matter. We could allow the owner of a closely held or family business to register her ownership interests within a Trust Account as a qualifying business. This would exempt the enterprise from the diversification rules. The taxing authorities would then have the right to audit the business periodically just as they do now, but the point of an audit would be to make sure that the business is not unfairly sheltering private consumption.

This issue arises commonly today under the inconsistent income tax, and it is especially problematic in the closely held or family business context. Employees should report as taxable income various types of special perks that they get from a business. If your company pays for your house or car, for example, you ought to pay tax on the fair rental value of what you use personally, even though many people don't report this kind of thing. But there are mechanisms in place to check on such abuse, and they would survive the transition to the Fair Not Flat Tax.

Like ownership interests in closely held and family businesses, stock in one's own company could be exempt, as it generally is now, from the diversification rules governing pension plans. For very wealthy people, such as Bill Gates and Warren Buffet, stock in their companies often represents a high percentage of their net worth. But their companies—Microsoft and Berkshire Hathaway—are regulated by the Securities and Exchange Commission, the relevant stock exchanges, and the Antitrust Department, as well as the IRS. These regulators are already on the lookout for excessive perks to key players within the companies. Under the Fair Not Flat Tax, we do not need to prevent such benefits; we only need to make sure that they get taxed. This issue is no different from ones that we have long faced under American law.

How can we distinguish nondeductible consumption from deductible savings?

A final set of hard cases for the definition of consumption concerns investments: what takes place inside the Trust Accounts. This is precisely parallel to the business-consumption problem we looked at above. For just as it is possible to smuggle consumption-type fun into the workplace, so might a taxpayer mix investment with pleasure.

Consider, for example, William Randolph Hearst—or Rupert Murdoch, for that matter—buying up newspapers (or sporting clubs, these days) partly as investments, and partly for the sheer fun of it. If we are taxing consumption but not investments, what do we do about these kinds of consumptive investments? This is another complex set of issues, but, again, they are ones we now face under the income tax. The bulk of capital in America is already regulated. Sensibly modified, rules such as the ones we have now can apply at least to large Trust Accounts.

Can we be concrete and specific for a moment? What would you say about investing in art? Is this consumption or not?

OK, let's see how this works in the case of a purchase of a work of art: the question is whether it constitutes savings. If it does, and if it takes place inside a Trust Account, you'll get a deduction for it. If it doesn't, you'll pay tax on the expense. When we understand the situation that way, we can see that there are sensible ways to approach purchases of art under the Fair Not Flat Tax.

First of all, we might want to include all art within a national sales tax or VAT, so everyone would pay at least the basic 10 percent sales tax on it; after all, there is some pleasure involved, and we wouldn't be able to administer a system that treated every poster hanging on a wall as art. Then comes the question of whether art is an investment allowable within Trust Accounts. Like most hard questions under the Fair Not Flat Tax, this one is left to the minority of Americans who consume enough to be subject to the supplemental personal consumption tax.

If we wanted to allow for the possibility that art could be deductible as an investment, we might create various rules. For example, we could set a minimum deductible purchase price, like $5,000 per item, so we wouldn't have to bother with lots of small cases. We might require that deductible art be registered and made available at certain times for public viewing—lent to an art museum, say. After all, the tax deduction is a matter of public largesse, so we might require some public-spiritedness of purchasers in order for them to obtain the deduction. This is akin to a charitable contribution deduction: art that is only to be hung in private mansions is fully taxable, art that is to be shared with the public is deductible. In this or some other way, we can create and monitor a distinction between art as an investment and art as an item of personal consumption and pleasure.

I don't mean this to be a definitive answer about how to treat art purchases under the Fair Not Flat Tax. I simply mean to illustrate the structure under which such a decision might be made. The basic principles of the Fair Not Flat Tax can guide us through a reasonable analysis in which many Americans might participate.

THE REALLY HARD PART: GETTING THERE

The greatest obstacles to change in our tax system lie in our political processes. A variety of factors—including the opposition of political partisans who may not fully understand tax in general or the reform idea in particular—make the political task of achieving the adoption of something like the Fair Not Flat Tax formidable. This concluding part addresses these matters.

Fears and Doubts about the Fair Not Flat Tax

If we don't tax savings at all, won't private capital build up and up, making the distribution of wealth more uneven than it is today?

Not necessarily, and probably not. Remember that the inconsistent income tax already fails to tax most savings. The estate tax is easily avoided by those so motivated. Worse, the rich today can consume tax free. Under a consistent spending tax, this will no longer be possible. A billionaire spending $10 million a year will now have to pay taxes on $10 million a year. The consistent progressive tax on spending will *reduce* the accumulated wealth of those rich people living the good life.

Here's another, more technical way to make the point. People often assume that tax rates will have to go up under a consumption tax, because the tax base will shrink when we systematically exclude savings. That would be true if we were we starting from a *consistent* income tax. But of course we are not. The inconsistent income tax already misses most savings. And a consistent consumption tax would have two major base-broadening features compared to the status quo: the inclusion of debt-financed consumption in the tax base, and the repeal of a special preference for capital gains. These changes would diminish, not enhance, the privileges of the rich.

But how can you just ignore the pleasure and power that large amounts of savings would bring?

This comment gets back to a basic liberal misconception: that fairness dictates taxing savings. I believe that the liberals are wrong.

For one thing, capital helps us all—perhaps especially the lower and middle classes. Rich people who are saving are contributing to society's overall well-being. They are not being selfish, spending every last penny on themselves in order to die broke. It's backward to have a tax policy that punishes rich people for saving and encourages them to spend—encourages them, that is, to pursue a lavish and luxurious lifestyle. High-end consumption, not the accumulation of capital, should be the liberal's true concern.

Let's take the liberal objection more seriously for a moment. It is true that large sums might build up in private Trust Accounts under a consistent consumption tax. But what is wrong with the mere possession of large amounts of wealth?

Two answers spring to mind. One, people who have wealth will one day be able to spend a lot of money on themselves and live luxuriously. The possession of wealth confers the right to future consumption. But a consistent progressive spending tax such as the Fair Not Flat Tax checks this problem. When holders of large Trust Accounts go to spend down their wealth, they will be taxed. If they make large withdrawals to spend lavishly on nonurgent needs, they will be taxed at the highest marginal rate level. The Fair Not Flat Tax gets at both actual consumption and future consumption. In fact, it does so far better than the inconsistent income tax system, notwithstanding the latter's seeming concern with capital as a source of potential consumption. Recall that when Ross Perot spent $60 million running for President, he *saved* $33 million in today's taxes. Under the proposed consistent consumption tax he would have to withdraw $120 million from his Trust Account and *pay* $60 million in taxes in order to spend $60 million on himself. Which system does a better job of getting at the pleasures that wealth bestows?

The second concern about the private possession of wealth is that people who have a lot of capital will become too powerful. Large pools of private savings may indeed confer a level of power on their holders that would be troubling in a liberal democracy. If Bill Gates or Warren Buffet could use their billions of dollars to affect politics, this would be problematic. Of course, they can do that easily enough under today's inconsistent income-plus-estate tax. Wealthy, sophisticated investors like Gates and Buffet need not pay any tax on their capital if they follow Artful Dodger's simple plan, even if they are using the money to influence economic markets or politics.

Liberals might point out that the Fair Not Flat Tax will allow even greater stores of wealth to accumulate within the Trust Accounts and hence will be more problematic than the status quo. I've already indicated my skepticism about this claim. But more important, a consistent spending tax automatically generates a mechanism to monitor and control the problem of the private abuse of wealth in a way that the current tax system does not. We can regulate the Trust Accounts to prevent their abuse just as we regulate most large pools of capital in America today.

What about the sheer joy and psychological pleasure of owning capital?

Some people may be happy just knowing that they have a large pool of savings. Millionaires next door seem to be like this—they value the financial independence and freedom that their savings confer on them and their families. To which my considered reply is: So what? We should wish that more, not fewer, of us would think and act this way.

By and large these wealthy savers have worked hard and saved well. They are entitled to the pleasures that come from these decisions. No tax tries to get at purely psychological pleasure. The inconsistent income tax leaves the spendthrift Grasshopper alone even though he enjoys whatever he is doing with his money. Die-brokers today can die happy and tax free. Why should we try to tax the pure pleasure that Ant gets from her savings? A consistent spending tax will tax her when and if she spends. Why isn't that enough? Why should we compel the millionaire next door to die sad, regretting that he didn't heed his financial planners' advice to die broke too?

How can the Fair Not Flat Tax ignore inheritances? Isn't it unfair that some people get to start life with a pile of money while most of us don't?

This question just reflects another confusion about tax. The Fair Not Flat Tax most definitely does not ignore inheritances. Far from it. The Fair Not Flat Tax does a much better job of meeting legitimate liberal concerns about inheritances than the half-baked system now in place.

Recall that Lear's prodigal daughters enjoyed the good life off of their father's wealth without paying any tax under today's rules. A tax-saving die-broke plan can easily involve early, frequent, and large gifts to potential heirs. Huge amounts of wealth can be passed tax free to spendthrift children under the inconsistent income-plus-estate tax. Under current law, it is the thrifty—like Ant and Cordelia—who are hit time and time again by the burden of taxes.

The Fair Not Flat Tax, in contrast, is quite systematic in getting at inheritances—but it gets at heirs' spending, not their mere possession of wealth. This is, after all, the consistent principle of the Fair Not Flat Tax: to tax spending and to leave work and savings—the mere possession of wealth—alone. Heirs will receive Trust Accounts tax free. When they withdraw and spend, they will be taxed. If they withdraw a lot to spend on nonurgent purchases, they will be taxed a lot. This is a far better—a more sensible, fair, simple, and efficient—means of taxing heirs than what we have now.

Labels can get in the way of sound analysis. An income-plus-estate tax sounds liberal, and a consumption-without-estate tax sounds conservative. But things aren't always as they seem. It is time for liberals especially to wake up and get it right.

Why don't we impose sumptuary taxes on luxuries as Adam Smith suggested?

Sumptuary taxes are specific rather than general, and as such they are complex, inefficient, and unfair. Under the administration of the first George Bush a luxury tax was put in place on things such as yachts, and it turned out to be a big mistake. People just stopped buying yachts; they had their old ones refurbished instead. Yacht builders started going out of business. This attracted media attention. Much to Bush's embarrassment, the tax had to be repealed. This story illustrates a general rule: because people can adjust to specific luxury taxes that pick and choose among goods and activities, these taxes often end up being counterproductive. But the Fair Not Flat Tax is a general and consistent spending tax, so it won't have these perverse effects. Yachts or luxury cars would be no more taxed or disfavored than any other item. It would all come down to each individual's or family's overall level of spending.

The Fair Not Flat Tax really isn't all that different from the current inconsistent income tax. The main difference is that it features a more systematic exemption for savings, or nonconsumption. This alone makes the whole tax system simpler, more efficient, and fairer. A consistent progressive spending tax allows us to make reasonable judgments about the appropriate levels of consumption at which to raise taxes. We don't have to pick and choose among particular items.

Wouldn't deductions for medical and educational expenses favor the rich, and therefore be unfair?

Possibly. This is a big part of the debate that we would have to have about allowing deductions, exemptions, and exclusions from a national sales tax, VAT, or supplemental personal consumption tax. It is true that an exemption for medical expenses is worth more for a high-bracket taxpayer than for a low-bracket taxpayer. But it isn't clear that this is the right way to think about things. The principled logic behind allowing a deduction for medical expenses is that regardless of income level people should only be taxed on what they spend for discretionary items of pleasure—which don't include emergency medical expenses. No one, rich or poor, should have to pay a tax on such costs.

I think this is a pretty compelling argument for making medical expenses, charitable contributions, and certain other expenses deductible. I think child care costs, for example, should be deductible as a business expense. I am less convinced when it comes to education, because in that case we might legitimately be worried about giving a more beneficial tax deduction to the rich. But my point in this book is not to resolve such issues once and for all. Rather, it is to show how they would be framed under a consistent consumption tax so the people can participate in discussions of tax policy. That's pretty much impossible now under today's inconsistent tax system. I hope more popular participation in discussions of tax policy will become almost common under the Fair Not Flat Tax.

If we carve out lots of exceptions under the Fair Not Flat Tax and do all of these other things you are suggesting, won't we get a complicated mess like we have now?

If the Fair Not Flat Tax became as complicated and exception riddled as our present system, tax reform would indeed be disappointing. But there are several reasons to believe that this worst-case scenario will not come to pass.

One, the systematic exclusion for savings will simplify the tax system a great deal. We saw in chapter 2 how much of the trouble with the income tax comes from the decision to tax savings, and what a mess the inconsistent commitment to doing so makes of the status quo.

Two, a national sales tax or VAT combined with a rebate mechanism would release tens of millions of Americans from the obligation of filling out complicated and intimidating tax forms every year. Whatever complexity is left will affect only a minority of Americans—families of four earning or spending more than $80,000 a year. Presumably, these families can afford some kind of tax assistance to help with the complexity they would face.

Three, the entire system would be governed by a set of clear and consistent principles. The foremost one is that we should tax spending, not work or savings. A second principle is that we should tax luxuries more than ordinaries, and ordinaries more than necessities. These principles are understandable to all parties—taxpayers, IRS officials, politicians, judges. So the system can be much more comprehensible than the current mess, whose principles are deeply hidden if they even exist.

Tax and Morality

How can the tax system make judgments about the morality of consumption choices? Isn't this illiberal and dictatorial?

This kind of objection rests on a misunderstanding of what the Fair Not Flat Tax is all about. The Fair Not Flat Tax is a general consumption tax—in essence, a progressive sales tax. The judgments it makes are general: that a family's first $20,000 of spending should be tax free, and that most spending by most Americans should bear a moderate tax, say at a 10 percent rate. The rich can afford to pay a somewhat higher rate, so in my preferred plan the supplemental personal consumption tax would kick in at spending above $80,000 or so.

Now that certainly isn't dictatorial. It also doesn't just come from my say-so. The rough Fair Not Flat Tax rate schedule is akin to what we have now under the inconsistent income tax and to what polls and experience have consistently shown that the American people support. Ever since 1913 we have had some progression in the major national tax levied on individuals. Most Americans think this is fair.

Certainly Americans who aren't wealthy don't want any major tax reform to involve a tax increase on them to pay for tax reduction for the rich.

But tax isn't a moral subject. We should have simple, neutral rules, not social engineering. A neutral flat tax is just what we need.

How can tax *not* be a moral subject? Tax tells us what we get to keep and what we have to give to the government. What would it mean to do that in a nonmoral way?

We've seen that a large liberal and progressive mistake in tax policy has been the foolish insistence on taxing capital or savings. A corresponding conservative error has been to cling to a naive belief in a neutral tax system. All taxes involve moral choices, the inconsistent income tax every bit as much as the Fair Not Flat Tax. The income tax, for example, makes a moral judgment about progressivity when it says that earnings above certain levels ought to be subject to higher tax rates. The problem lies not in the fact that a moral judgment is being made; the problem is that this is the wrong moral judgment to make, because earnings are the wrong thing to be judging. A consistent income tax would be a double tax on savers, like the thrifty Ant, and a consistent-income-plus-effective-estate tax would be a triple tax on thrifty intergenerational savers, like King Lear and most millionaires next door. Those are moral judgments. They are also bad ones.

People who object to morality in tax are deluding themselves. They often want a flat tax because it sounds neutral. But it's not. For one thing, the proposed flat taxes all have two rate brackets—a large zero bracket or exemption level and a single rate on the rest of income or consumption. The zero bracket reflects a moral decision about the importance or urgency of low-end spending. But even if we had a truly flat tax, this would reflect a moral decision that all levels of earnings—or spending as the case may be—are equally appropriate to tax.

Tax systems also reflect decisions about *what* to tax, and here also the quest for neutrality is misguided. Whether levied on income or consumption, consistent taxes are all arguably neutral—one kind taxes all income, from whatever source derived; the other all spending, regardless of where the money comes from. Which is better? That's a moral question, and an invocation of "neutrality" isn't going to supply an answer to it. Likewise, either tax can sustain deductions for certain uses, such as medical expenses and charitable contributions. Once more, the mantra of neutrality isn't going to get us out of the need to make these hard choices.

There is no way to avoid facing the morality of tax. We could turn the whole mess over to technocrats or politicians or whomever, but both the decision to have others do the dirty work and the kind of dirty work these others do would entail moral choices. So we might as well be honest and admit that we are making moral decisions. Then we can devote our full attention to trying to make fair and sensible ones.

But isn't consumption a right of the earner?

I find that the language of rights is generally misplaced when it comes to tax. The fact of the matter is that America now taxes one-third of its GDP—almost $3 trillion a year goes to the federal, state, and local tax collectors. The government takes that money, and you go to jail if you try to get out of paying it. This is simply a brute fact of modern life. Tax tells you what is private and what is public, what you get to keep and what you have to send in to the government.

The Fair Not Flat Tax doesn't change any of the basic facts of tax; it doesn't in and of itself change the size of the total tax burden. All the Fair Not Flat Tax does is to alter the activity being taxed: we would make judgments about spending instead of about work and savings. Asserting that one has a right to use one's earnings as one sees fit doesn't add anything meaningful to the analysis under today's tax or tomorrow's.

Taking the Final Steps

Isn't the Fair Not Flat Tax too complicated?

I hope not. That's why I have written this book, after all—because I believe that the American people can understand the Fair Not Flat Tax. It looks a lot like the Nunn-Domenici USA Tax, discussed in chapter 3, which was proposed in 1995 and was widely considered infeasible because of its complexity. But I have learned from the criticism of the USA plan and have tried to fashion a tax that is less complicated and whose complexities will affect only a small minority of the public.

Conceptually, the Fair Not Flat Tax is a consistent, progressive spending tax—nothing more. Most Americans can understand the associated principles. The large majority of Americans will no longer have to fill out intimidating forms and will need only pay the relatively simple national sales tax or VAT. Only the wealthy will need to bother with the supplemental personal consumption tax, and although this undeniably has its complexities, it is certainly no worse—and I believe it is a good deal better—than the current disaster of the inconsistent income-plus-estate tax.

The fact that the entire tax system will rest on a clear and consistent set of principles—tax people as they spend, not as they work or save; tax luxuries more than ordinaries, and ordinaries more than necessities—represents an enormous improvement over the status quo. These principles form the heart and soul of the Fair Not Flat Tax. And they are not terribly complicated.

What about the actual transition? Can we ever get from here to there?

Yes, I think we can. I address the topic of change briefly in chapter 6. Lots of people—academics, lobbyists, politicians—get bogged down in questions of transitions, and pretty soon things start looking hopeless. In this book I wanted to put first things first. I set out the principles, hoping to get all readers to a point where they could see a way through to a consistent, progressive spending tax with most people off of the official tax rolls. No doubt getting there will be hard, and many issues will come up—including many that I have not discussed or even anticipated. But it will be worth it.

We ought to start with a clear sense of how bad things are, and they are very bad indeed. Our current fiscal good health—the presence of a federal surplus (perhaps?)—gives us room to maneuver. Before we go too far down the road of making small, ad hoc changes to a badly flawed system, we ought to think of paying the short-term price of transition to a better one. The long-term benefits are there for the taking.

What will be the big practical problems in transition?

Certainly starting up a national sales tax or VAT presents formidable administrative and other problems—as commencing any new tax does. Figuring out how to collect the tax and monitor its collection will be difficult. Likewise, the rebate mechanism will need to go through a period of trial and error.

But the general conversion from an inconsistent income to a consistent consumption tax may not be as difficult as is often feared. First off, we are already so far down the path toward having a consumption tax that this really isn't a radical shift. We already have the IRA mechanism in place; the Trust Accounts simply involve an unlimited expansion of this model. Because we would be raising its zero bracket or exemption level dramatically, few taxpayers would have to worry about the most complicated aspects of the supplemental personal consumption tax or the attendant filling out of forms. The biggest practical problems will most likely involve reporting debt on the D-2 forms and resolving the question of what to do about preenactment basis, as I discussed in the chapter 6. Of course, a flat-out repeal of the gift and estate tax will bring about significant simplification in that area. The lingering complexity will be in the registration of Trust Accounts, but given Social Security numbers and modern technology, this ought not to be too difficult.

I'm just about sold on the Fair Not Flat Tax Plan, but I fear that you're ignoring too many details.

Perhaps I am. I don't think so, though. This is a book mainly about forests, not about trees or shrubs or weeds, of which there are many in tax. I have tried to think through and anticipate most of the details, questions, and objections, and I hope that I have conveyed many of these thoughts, at least briefly, here. The Further Reading section that follows provides suggestions for those who are interested in learning more. But I have always thought that it is important to get the big picture down first or nothing will ever happen: we'll live with a complicated, inconsistent, incoherent, ineffective, and unfair tax system forever.

It's time to fix tax. I believe that we can. I hope that we will.

GLOSSARY OF KEY TERMS

APPRECIATION. The rise in value of an asset. Appreciation can be due to inflation or can represent a real gain in value. Appreciation is not consistently taxed under the current inconsistent income tax.

AFTER-TAX DOLLARS. Dollars that have already been taxed. If you earn $10,000 at work and your taxes come to $1,500, you are left with $8,500 in after-tax dollars. You should not be taxed on this amount again. *See also* basis.

AVERAGE TAX RATE. The tax rate that an average dollar bears in taxes. Under an income tax, the average tax rate is calculated by dividing one's total taxes by one's total income. *See also* marginal tax rate.

BASE. *See* tax base.

BASIS. After-tax dollars. If you invest with money that has already been subject to the income tax, you have basis in the investment equal to its cost: that value cannot be taxed again. Roth IRAs have basis because the contributions to fund them are not tax deductible. If, on the other hand, you get a tax deduction for an investment, you have no basis in the investment, so its value can still be subject to an income tax. Traditional IRAs do not have basis because the contributions to them are tax deductible. The current income tax allows one to receive certain types of income tax free: cash gifts, tax-exempt interest, the proceeds of life insurance, and so on. Because you are not supposed to ever pay tax on such items, they have basis. *See also* after-tax dollars; carryover basis; stepped-up basis.

BUILT-IN GAIN. Appreciation that has not yet been taxed. If you buy a share of stock for $100 and it rises in value to $150, you will have $50 of built-in gain, also called unrealized appreciation.

CAPITAL ASSET. Property that has been held for over one year. Investments can be capital assets; inventory and certain self-created assets, such as books and paintings in the hands of writers and artists, cannot.

CAPITAL APPRECIATION. The rise in value of a capital asset.

CAPITAL GAIN OR LOSS. The tax gain or loss that is realized when a capital asset is sold.

CAPITAL GAINS TAX RATE. The tax rate applied to a capital gain or loss. The capital gains tax rate is lower than the rate applied to ordinary income; currently it stands at a maximum of 20 percent, much lower than the top rate of 39.6 percent (as I write) for ordinary income. *See also* ordinary income.

CARRYOVER BASIS. The basis that a new owner of an asset takes over from its prior owner under certain transactions, most importantly those involving gifts. If Jack buys stock for $100, it appreciates in value to $150, and Jack then gives the stock to Jill as a gift, Jill will take a carryover basis of $100 in the stock. In this way, both the basis and the built-in gain stay with the stock and its new owner. *See also* basis; built-in gain.

CASH-FLOW TAX. A postpaid consumption, or spending, tax.

CONSUMER DURABLE. A consumption item that lasts over time, like a house or a car.

CONSUMPTION. Income or wealth that is spent rather than saved. According to the Haig-Simons definition, Consumption = Income − Savings.

CONSUMPTION TAX. Any broad-based, comprehensive tax on a person's flow of funds that does not directly fall on savings. *See also* Haig-Simons definition.

CREDIT. A dollar-for-dollar reduction in tax owed. If for example you are eligible for a per-child tax credit, your tax owed (not your taxable income) is reduced by $500 per child. Unlike deductions, which subtract from taxable income, credits are not regressive: they are (at least if they are refundable) worth the same dollar amounts to all taxpayers. *Compare* deduction. *See also* nonrefundable rebates and credits; refundable rebates and credits.

CREDIT-INVOICE VAT. A value-added tax levied on gross receipts and combined with a credit for taxes demonstrably paid by suppliers. This is the form of VAT most commonly used around the world. *See also* value-added tax; subtraction-method VAT.

DEDUCTION. A subtraction from the tax base. Under the present system, if you make charitable contributions worth $10,000, you can deduct this amount from your otherwise taxable income; that amount of your income will not be taxed. Deductions have a regressive effect in a progressive system: they are worth more to taxpayers in high marginal tax rate brackets. *Compare* credit.

DEATH TAX. *See* gift and estate tax.

EFFECTIVE TAX RATE. *See* average tax rate.

ESTATE TAX. *See* gift and estate tax.

EXEMPTION LEVEL. *See* zero bracket.

FAIR NOT FLAT TAX. My term for a consistent, progressive, postpaid consumption, or spending, tax. Such a general type of tax can take several different practical forms, but my preferred version combines a national sales tax or VAT with a supplemental personal consumption tax for high-end spenders.

FLAT TAX. Literally, a tax that imposes a single rate or sum on all taxpayers. In practice, all modern flat-tax proposals involve two rates because they feature some kind of exemption level or zero bracket. *See also* zero bracket.

401(k) PLAN. A tax-favored pension plan that allows its holder to deduct the amount of contributions from otherwise taxable income. The tax on these plans works like a postpaid consumption tax: it falls due when the money is withdrawn to be spent, not when it is initially earned. *See* postpaid consumption tax.

GIFT AND ESTATE TAX. A tax that falls on one who transfers wealth. The gift tax falls on the living gift giver; the estate tax falls on the estate of the deceased wealth holder. The gift and estate tax is also called the unified wealth transfer system or, colloquially, the death tax. In current practice, few persons pay any gift tax, because of its generous exemption levels; the gift and estate tax is in effect a tax on the net wealth of the richest decedents.

HAIG-SIMONS DEFINITION. The principle that Income = Consumption + Savings, named after the economists Robert Haig and Henry Simons. Note that the definition can be rearranged to serve as one for consumption: Consumption = Income − Savings.

HEAD TAX. A tax that imposes a flat or lump sum on every individual.

INCOME. According to the Haig-Simons definition, Consumption + Savings.

INCOME TAX. A tax on both consumption and savings.

INFLATION. The general rise in a price level.

INDEXING FOR INFLATION. Adjusting a price or other monetary value so that it uses real, or inflation-adjusted, values. For example, a zero bracket indexed for inflation will increase periodically to reflect the rate of inflation. If inflation is 5 percent, a $10,000 bracket for Year 1 will become a $10,500 bracket in Year 2.

IRA. Individual Retirement Account, a tax-favored savings account that—in its "traditional" form—operates on a postpaid consumption tax model: savers deposit pretax dollars and don't pay taxes until they withdraw the money. *See also* Roth IRA.

LOCK-IN EFFECT. The present law's tendency to discourage the sale of capital assets that have built-in gain. The lock-in effect breeds inefficiency because wealth holders retain assets that might otherwise be sold to persons who value them more highly.

LUMP SUM TAX. *See* head tax.

MARGINAL TAX RATE. The rate of tax one pays on the next dollar of income. If a taxpayer is in the 28 percent marginal tax bracket and earns $1,000 next week, she will pay a tax of $280 on those earnings. *See also* average tax rate.

NATIONAL RETAIL SALES TAX. *See* sales tax.

NONREFUNDABLE REBATE OR CREDIT. A rebate or credit limited to the amount of taxes paid. For example, the $500 per-child tax credit under current law is nonrefundable. If a taxpayer with two children owes only $800 in taxes before the credit is applied, her tax will be reduced to zero but not below; she will not benefit from the additional $200 of the credit. *See also* credit; rebate; refundable rebate or credit.

NUNN-DOMENICI PLAN. *See* USA Tax.

ORDINARY INCOME. Income from wages, interest, dividends, and other usual inflows. Ordinary income does not include proceeds from the sale of capital assets. *See also* capital gain or loss.

PAYROLL TAX. A tax levied on labor earnings and typically remitted by the employer. The Social Security and Medicare contribution system is the leading example.

PENSION PLAN. A retirement savings vehicle, typically maintained or established by one's employer, that is tax-favored under present law.

POLL TAX. *See* head tax.

POSTPAID CONSUMPTION TAX. A tax levied when money is spent, not when it is earned or saved. A sales tax is a leading example. The Fair Not Flat Tax also follows this form of tax.

PREENACTMENT BASIS. The basis in an asset held prior to the start of a new tax system. There is no general need for the concept of basis under the Fair Not Flat Tax, so policymakers will have to decide what to do about dollars that were taxed and saved before the transition to the Fair Not Flat Tax. *See also* basis.

PREPAID CONSUMPTION TAX. A tax that falls on income when it is earned, but not on the yield to savings. Also called a wage tax. Payroll taxes, such as the Social Security contribution, are a leading example. Most common flat-tax proposals follow this form of tax.

PROGRESSIVE TAX. A system of taxation in which higher earners or spenders pay a higher average tax rate than lower earners or spenders. *See also* average tax rate; flat tax; regressive tax.

RATE. *See* tax rate.

RATE BRACKET. The range of income over which a certain marginal tax rate applies. If the marginal rate is 15 percent for earnings between $10,000 and $30,000, a taxpayer will pay 15 percent on every dollar she earns over $10,000 but under $30,000.

RATE SCHEDULE. The full range of tax rates and rate brackets in a tax system.

REAL VALUE. Value that is held constant over time. Real value reflects actual purchasing power. Because of inflation, a coat that you can buy for $100 in Year 1 will cost more the following year. The real value of your dollars will have declined.

REALIZATION REQUIREMENT. The rule that an asset holder need not pay tax until the asset is sold or exchanged—until the underlying built-in gain is realized. *See also* built-in gain.

REBATE. The return of a tax that has already been paid.

REFUNDABLE REBATE OR CREDIT. A rebate or credit that can exceed the amount of taxes paid. The present Earned Income Tax Credit, the linchpin of the government's "workfare" support, is refundable. If a taxpayer owes $800 in taxes before the credit is applied, and her credit is $1,000, she will receive a refund of $200. *See also* credit; rebate; nonrefundable rebate or credit.

REGRESSIVE TAX. A system in which higher earners or spenders pay a lower average tax rate than lower earners or spenders. *See also* average tax rate; flat tax; progressive tax.

ROLLOVER PROVISIONS. Rules under the current income tax whereby built-in gain can be transferred from one asset to another without triggering tax. *See also* basis; built-in gain.

ROTH IRA. An Individual Retirement Account that operates on the prepaid consumption tax model: savers deposit after-tax dollars and do not pay taxes on withdrawals. *See also* IRA; prepaid consumption tax.

SALES TAX. A tax levied on consumer purchases, typically collected from sellers but borne effectively by buyers.

SAVINGS. Nonconsumed, or unspent, wealth. Income − Consumption under the Haig-Simons definition of income.

STEPPED-UP BASIS. An adjustment of basis to fair market value, which the current income tax grants for assets acquired after a death. A decedent might have had only $1,000 of basis in an investment valued at $10,000; when his heirs receive the asset, it will have a new basis matching its current fair market value—$10,000. *See also* basis; carryover basis.

SUBTRACTION-METHOD VAT. A form of value-added tax that is levied on gross receipts minus the cost of purchased inputs. This is the most commonly proposed form for an American VAT. *See also* credit-invoice VAT; value-added tax.

SUPPLEMENTAL PERSONAL CONSUMPTION TAX. Under my preferred Fair Not Flat Tax plan, a tax on high-end spenders that will supplement a national sales tax or VAT.

TAXABLE UNIT. The *who* of taxation; the person or persons responsible for paying a tax. The taxable unit can be an individual, a married couple, a household, and so on.

TAX BASE. The *what* of taxation; the value subject to tax. Income is the base of an income tax; purchased goods and services are the base of most sales taxes.

TAX RATE. The *how much* of taxation; the percentage of a tax base that is collected by the government. *See also* average tax rate; marginal tax rate.

TRUST ACCOUNT. The term I am using for a nontaxable savings account under the Fair Not Flat Tax. A Trust Account would be similar to a traditional IRA under current law and to the Unlimited Savings Allowances under the Nunn-Domenici tax reform proposal.

UNREALIZED APPRECIATION. *See* built-in gain.

USA TAX PLAN. A proposal by then Senators Nunn and Domenici for an individual, progressive, postpaid consumption tax featuring Unlimited Savings Allowances that are akin to the traditional IRAs under current law and the Trust Accounts under my proposed Fair Not Flat Tax plan.

VALUE-ADDED TAX (VAT). A tax levied on the value added at different stages of a production process; in essence, a sales tax that is collected gradually. *See also* credit-invoice VAT; subtraction-method VAT.

YIELD-EXEMPT TAX. A prepaid consumption tax, like the Social Security contribution system, that taxes wages but subsequently ignores the yield to savings. *See also* prepaid consumption tax.

ZERO BRACKET. The amount of a tax base not subject to tax.

FURTHER READING

If you're interested in learning more, here are some sources that will provide a good start.

CLASSICS

Kaldor, Nicholas. *An Expenditure Tax*. London: Allen & Unwin, 1955. An early and brilliant exposition of the nature of and case for a cash-flow, or postpaid, consumption tax.

Mill, John Stuart. *Principles of Political Economy*. 1848. Reprint, edited by J. Riley, Oxford: Oxford University Press, 1994. Mill was perhaps the greatest writer in the tradition of political economists who freely mixed philosophy, economics, and politics. Here he articulates the case against income taxation and sets out the double-tax criticism.

Musgrave, Richard. *The Theory of Public Finance: A Study in Public Economy*. New York: McGraw-Hill, 1959. One of the seminal texts in public finance by a major economist.

Simons, Henry Calvert. *Federal Tax Reform*. Chicago: University of Chicago Press, 1950. Also *Personal Income Taxation: The Definition of Income as a Problem of Fiscal Policy*. Chicago: University of Chicago Press, 1938. Simons was the major conceptual thinker behind the income tax, and his two books retain much historic interest.

Smith, Adam. *An Inquiry into the Nature and Causes of the Wealth of Nations*. 1776. Reprint, edited by Edwin Cannan, Modern Library, New York: Random House, 1965. This remains a wonderful volume. Book 5 considers taxes. Smith is important not only as an early pioneer of free market theory, but also for his general method and his approach to questions of public policy. Smith and his colleagues of the Scottish Enlightenment, such as David Hume, were skeptical of overly idealistic theory and made a point of paying careful attention to human nature and practical politics. Smith's observations on taxation reflect these traits.

WORKS OF THE 1970S AND 1980S

Aaron, Henry J., Harvey Galper, and Joseph A. Pechman, eds., *Uneasy Compromise: Problems of a Hybrid Income-Consumption Tax*. Washington, D.C.: Brookings Institution, 1988. A helpful and interesting collection of essays by leading public-finance economists and tax-law scholars.

Birnbaum, Jeffrey H., and Alan S. Murray. *Showdown at Gucci Gulch: Lawmakers, Lobbyists, and the Unlikely Triumph of Tax Reform*. New York: Vintage Books, 1987. A thorough, interesting, and highly readable account of the making of the Tax Reform Act of 1986, written by two veteran *Wall Street Journal* writers.

Bittker, Boris. *Collected Legal Essays*. Littleton, Co.: F. B. Rothman, 1989. Bittker is the greatest American tax-law academic, and this volume contains all of his many impressive writings on the income tax, composed over a nearly forty-year period starting in the 1950s.

Bradford, David F. *Untangling the Income Tax*. Cambridge: Harvard University Press, 1986. A lucid exposition of how the income tax works, by a leading public economist who has often been critical of the tax.

Bradford, David F. and the U.S. Treasury Tax Policy Staff. *Blueprints for Basic Tax Reform*, 2d ed., rev. Arlington, Va.: Tax Analysts, 1984. This book came out of President Ford's Treasury Department's study of transitions to a consumption tax (the first edition appeared in 1977). It is enormously interesting and well-researched.

Bradley, Bill. *The Fair Tax*. New York: Pocket Books, 1984. A very clear, well-written account of one view of the problems of the tax system in the early 1980s, this is an important exposition and defense of the strategy behind the Tax Reform Act of 1986: to improve the income tax by broadening its base and lowering its rates.

Cooper, George. *A Voluntary Tax? New Perspectives on Sophisticated Estate Tax Avoidance*. Washington, D.C.: Brookings Institution, 1979. A report of tax avoidance strategies under the estate tax in the mid-1970s. Many of the particulars are dated, but the fundamental things still apply as time goes by.

RECENT TITLES

Adams, Charles. *Those Dirty Rotten Taxes*. New York: The Free Press, 1998. A polemical but vivid account of past and present antitax attitudes in America.

Atkinson, Anthony B. *Public Economics in Action: The Basic Income/Flat Tax Proposal*. New York: Oxford University Press, 1995. A fairly accessible treatment of modern tax reform options by one of today's most sophisticated public finance economists.

Bartlett, Donald L., and James B. Steele. *The Great American Tax Dodge: How Spiraling Fraud and Avoidance Are Killing Fairness, Destroying the Income Tax, and Costing You*. Boston: Little, Brown, 2000. An occasionally overwritten account of aggressive tax planning and cheating under the individual and corporate income taxes.

Frank, Robert H. *Luxury Fever: Why Money Fails to Satisfy in an Era of Excess*.

New York: The Free Press, 1999. A leading psychological economist presses the argument that Americans are spending too much for their own good, caught up in a vicious cycle of luxury spending. Frank recommends a progressive consumption tax similar to the Fair Not Flat Tax as the social solution to the problems of too much high-end consumption and too little savings.

Graetz, Michael J. *The Decline (and Fall?) of the Income Tax.* New York: W. W. Norton, 1997. A colorful account of the tax system and policymaking today and in the recent past, by a leading tax-law professor and former high-ranking Treasury Department official.

Hall, Robert, and Alvin Rabushka. *The Flat Tax,* 2nd ed. Stanford, Calif.: Hoover Institution Press, Stanford University, 1995. The seminal treatise on the flat tax, by two academics. Concise and informative.

Kiyosaki, Robert T., with Sharon L. Lechter. *Rich Dad, Poor Dad: What the Rich Teach Their Kids about Money—That the Poor and Middle Class Do Not!* New York: Warner, 1997. The best-selling guide to life and finances in modern American that I have quoted liberally throughout. Rich Dad is a high-asset-holding, low-tax-paying capitalist while Poor Dad is a highly taxed wage earner, reflecting what I take as our backward tax policy today.

McCaffery, Edward J. *Taxing Women.* Chicago: University of Chicago Press, 1997. My book about how the U.S. tax system affects women, especially married working mothers, and two-earner families.

McCaffery, Edward J. "The Uneasy Case for Wealth Transfer Taxation." *Yale Law Journal* 283 (1994). Also "The Political Liberal Case against the Estate Tax." *Philosophy and Public Affairs* 281 (1994). Two scholarly articles setting out my case against the estate tax and developing the argument for a consistent, progressive consumption tax.

Pollack, Sheldon David. *The Failure of U.S. Tax Policy: Revenue and Politics.* University Park: Pennsylvania State University Press, 1996. A thorough, helpful, and interesting survey and analysis of the making of recent U.S. tax policy, written by a former tax lawyer who is now an academic.

Pollan, Stephen M., and Mark Levine. *Die Broke: A Radical, Four-Part Financial Plan.* New York: HarperCollins, 1997. Investment advice about how to enjoy your wealth while you're alive and leave nothing when you're on your deathbed, avoiding the onerous gift and estate tax discussed in chapter 5.

Seidman, Laurence. *The USA Tax.* Cambridge, Mass.: MIT Press, 1997. An excellent treatment of the Nunn-Domenici USA Tax plan and related models, with a few technical criticisms and objections, written by a public finance economist.

Shlaes, Amity. *The Greedy Hand: How Taxes Drive Honest Americans Crazy and What to Do about It.* New York: Random House, 1999. A highly readable and entertaining account of current American attitudes toward tax, written by an editorial writer then at the *Wall Street Journal.*

Slemrod, Joel, and Jon Bakija, *Taxing Ourselves,* 2d ed. Cambridge, Mass.: MIT Press, 2000. A fairly accessible account of the current tax system and its chief competitors, written by two important public finance economists.

Stanley, Thomas J., and William D. Danko, *The Millionaire Next Door: The Sur-*

prising Secrets of America's Wealthy. Atlanta, Ga.: Longstreet, 1996. An extended study, based on surveys, interviews, published data, and other sources, of the lifestyles of America's millionaires. It paints a general picture of a thrifty and frugal class of people who are concerned with financial independence and generally not interested in ostentation or luxury.

Sullivan, Martin A., and the American Institute of Certified Public Accountants. *America's Tax Revolution: How It Will Affect You* and *Changing America's Tax System: A Guide to the Debate.* New York: John Wiley, 1996. Two volumes, the first of which is longer and somewhat more technical, authored by leading public accountants. Extremely helpful in their analysis of many of the details of the competing tax reform proposals and in their focus on issues of transition and compliance.

INDEX

Terms in bold type are defined in the glossary.